SCREEN-FREE
FUN

······· *Shannon Philpott-Sanders* ·······

400 Activities for the Whole Family

Adams Me

New York   London   Toronto   Sydney   New Delhi

Adams Media
An Imprint of Simon & Schuster, Inc.
57 Littlefield Street
Avon, Massachusetts 02322

First Adams Media trade paperback edition APRIL 2018

ADAMS MEDIA and colophon are trademarks of Simon and Schuster.

For information about special discounts for bulk purchases, please contact Simon & Schuster Special Sales at 1-866-506-1949 or business@ simonandschuster.com.

The Simon & Schuster Speakers Bureau can bring authors to your live event. For more information or to book an event contact the Simon & Schuster Speakers Bureau at 1-866-248-3049 or visit our website at www.simon speakers.com.

Interior design by Colleen Cunningham

Manufactured in the United States of America

10 9 8 7 6 5 4 3 2

Library of Congress Cataloging-in-Publication Data has been applied for.

ISBN 978-1-5072-0599-0
ISBN 978-1-5072-0600-3 (ebook)

Readers are urged to take all appropriate precautions before undertaking any how-to task. Always read and follow instructions and safety warnings for all tools and materials, and call in a professional if the task stretches your abilities too far. Although every effort has been made to provide the best possible information in this book, neither the publisher nor the author is responsible for accidents, injuries, or damage incurred as a result of tasks undertaken by readers. This book is not a substitute for professional services.

Acknowledgments

This book would not have been possible without the support of my husband, children, family, and friends. While I spent months brainstorming ideas to keep families entertained, I had the support of my husband, John, who picked up the slack in our home of seven, and offered me the emotional support I desperately needed. Our four children, Paige, Joel, Jacilyn, and Josh, were instrumental in providing me with not only ideas, but also the inspiration to write as I thought about the childhood games they took part in so willingly. Our two-year-old grandson, Levi, game me the motivation to identify activities that would help him stay off the screen and burn off all of the endless energy he has at every waking moment. And I can't forget the support of our two dogs, Chance and Rudy, who camped out by my feet while I was writing into the wee hours of the night.

In addition, my extended family was instrumental in helping me write this book. Thank you to my mother, Linda Basnett, and stepdad, Jerry Basnett, for reading through each chapter and reminding me of some of my favorite activities as a kid. Thank you to my in-laws, Jerry and Karen Sanders, for staying up late with me to brainstorm their favorite activities as kids while visiting from Texas. My sisters, Dana Jaenke and Molly Hayden, offered me encouragement when I worried I was out of ideas, and my aunts, uncles, cousins, nieces, and nephews were also there to offer me a pat on the back when I needed it.

I wrote this book because I truly believe in the benefit of expressing your creativity, staying active outdoors, and giving back to your community without the help of technology. My childhood was filled with creative activities well before cell phones and the Internet even existed and I look back fondly at these memories. My hope is that you and your children can make some memories that will last a lifetime while trying out these four hundred activities together.

Contents

INTRODUCTION / 13

1. EMBRACE YOUR CREATIVITY / 15

4. PUT A FUN TWIST ON LOCAL TRAVEL / 171

Introduction

You probably envisioned your children growing up like you did, exploring the great outdoors, playing all sorts of imaginative games, and crafting adorable projects. However, what you may notice instead is that those giggles in the backyard are nonexistent and your children are either glued to their tablets or complaining that they're bored.

Although technology has enhanced the way children learn and socialize, extreme amounts of screen time can make creative play more of a challenge for them. Even worse, it reduces the amount of physical exercise they get. The more often you replace a few minutes of screen time with creative activities, the more comfortable your child will feel being imaginative and silly. Just like with any skill, you have to practice to become proficient.

If you're ready to limit screen time, put away the smartphones, and teach your children how to have fun without a gadget, this is the book for you. Make rainy afternoons at home and long trips in the car much more interesting with the ideas in this book. Instead of turning to screens to fill some time, offer an alternative that gets the entire family involved in games, activities, and crafts. With four designated sections to provide your family with interesting ways to bond and spend time together, you can choose just the right activity to make the most of your precious time together:

- **GET CREATIVE:** Help your children embrace their creativity with one hundred ways of turning simple household products into artwork worthy of hanging on the fridge.
- **GET ACTIVE (AND SOMETIMES A LITTLE MESSY):** Exercise your entire family's bodies and minds with one hundred ways to get to know the great outdoors, whether it's sunny or snowy.

- **GIVE BACK:** Teach your children the value of helping others with one hundred activities designed to give back to your local community.
- **HAVE FUN:** When your children get restless on a long road trip or an impromptu excursion (or even if you're just stuck at home on a rainy afternoon), dig into the one hundred ways offered here to put a fun twist on travel (or nontravel!).

Show your kids that they—and you!—don't need TV, video games, or handheld electronics to have a good time. Each activity includes an age range, but feel free to use your best judgment as to which activities are suitable based on your children's abilities, interests, and personalities. You'll also see a level of difficulty with each entry, which indicates how involved the activity is, in terms of necessary materials, travel, adult participation, and so on:

■☐☐ = beginner
■■☐ = intermediate
■■■ – advanced

Let's bring those giggles back to the center of your home, get fit, rediscover the joy in family trips, and support your community—together, and without screens!

1. EMBRACE YOUR CREATIVITY

Get ready to get messy, silly, and colorful when embarking on these one hundred activities that prompt your kids to think outside of the (cardboard) box. From weaving bracelets to making cotton ball snowmen, adventure is right around the corner when you make arts and crafts a part of your weekly routine. Got a young artist? Make wax paper placemats. Is your kid's imagination just waiting to be tapped? Have him draft a comic strip or form a poetry club. Or watch as your kids turn into musicians with homemade music shakers. Using mainly basic household supplies—such as toothpicks, paper towel rolls, shoe boxes, paper, and pens—you can have an activity ready to go the moment your child says "I'm boooored." Find fun-filled playtime activities that the entire family can enjoy (while inside or outside!)—many of which do not require an adult's constant supervision.

○ WEAVE A FRIENDSHIP BRACELET

Scour your craft or sewing supplies for thread or yarn and use it to show your children how to weave simple bracelets. This is an easily customizable activity that's great for just one child or an entire group of kids. The bracelets give them a way to express their creativity and add colorful accessories to their wardrobe or as tokens to exchange with friends. Have each child choose the colors of yarn or thread he prefers and cut them into strips of the same size (about 30 inches to make a 6-inch bracelet). Gather the strips, tie a knot on one end, and tape the knot to a surface to hold it steady (anchor it to something that the tape won't damage). Then help your kids weave, braid, or twist the thread or yarn into whatever pattern they prefer. Once the bracelet is long enough, knot the other end. Tie the ends together and you have a bracelet! Encourage your children to mix and match colors or even attach sequins to the bracelets with a dab of glue for added sparkle and shine.

○ CRAFT PERSONALIZED NOTEBOOKS

Do you have a bunch of partially used notebooks hanging around? Give them new life by decorating the covers. Get started by gathering pens, markers, glue, stickers, glitter, and construction paper. Ask your children to visualize the perfect notebook and then help them make it a reality. The possibilities are endless, but here are a few ideas to help you get started: cut construction paper into shapes and glue them onto the notebook; arrange stickers to make a fun scene; drip glue on the cover and scatter glitter over the wet glue to create a sparkling design; or take personalization to another level by taping or gluing personal photos on the notebook. The sky is the limit!

○ MAKE PANCAKE ART

Dealing with tired or bored kids at breakfast on Sunday? Get your children involved in preparing the meal while also entertaining them by turning a routine morning meal into a decorated treat. Mix up your favorite pancake batter recipe, and then arm your children with spoons, spatulas, and toothpicks to begin creating works of art. Pour a small amount of batter into a pan away from the stove or onto a griddle that has not yet heated up and have your kids form shapes with the batter. For instance, they can use a spoon or spatula to shape the batter into letters or animals, and they can use a toothpick to add small details such as eyes, a nose, and a smiling mouth complete with teeth. Fire up the stove or griddle and cook the piece of art for your children.

○ BUILD A PLAYING CARD TOWER

If your kids are bored with traditional card games, give them a platform to make their own architectural structures. With just a few decks of cards you can entertain them and enhance their concentration skills. Once your children are equipped with at least one deck of cards, instruct them how to stack the cards. Make a pyramid or a rectangular house with the cards situated both vertically and horizontally. If your children want a permanent structure, put some glue on the ends of each card as they build.

○ CRAFT STUFFED-ANIMAL BEDS

Even stuffed animals need a comfortable place to sleep. If your child's bed is cluttered with plush toys, spend an afternoon crafting beds so they both can sleep more comfortably. All you need is a few shoe boxes or shipping boxes to accommodate these stuffed creatures. Find the perfect box for each stuffed animal's size and then let the decorating begin. Break out some construction paper to tape onto the sides of the boxes and crayons for your children to decorate the "beds." You can also attach stickers to the sides of the boxes or label each "bed" with the stuffed animal's name. Next, gather small blankets (baby receiving blankets work well), cotton balls, or even newspapers to create a soft space for their treasured friends. Little ones may enjoy putting their animals down for a nap by singing a lullaby or reading a book once the stuffed animals are tucked into their new beds.

○ SKETCH A FAVORITE CHARACTER

Bring your child's favorite cartoon characters to life with a sketching session. Start by asking your child to make a list of her favorite characters from TV or movies. Then, find a picture from a book that she can replicate in a sketchbook or on a blank piece of paper. Make the task easier for younger children by placing a picture of a cartoon character underneath a transparent piece of paper so they can easily trace the outline of the head and body before filling it in with markers or crayons. Encourage older children to practice their freehand skills instead of tracing. Add an extra level of fun to the activity by hosting a contest and creating awards for everyone, such as Most Creative Sketch or Most Colorful Cartoon Character.

○ MAKE SOME GLITTERY SLIME

You can easily make cool-looking slime that kids of all ages like to play with by mixing together just two inexpensive ingredients. In a small bowl, combine ¼ cup glitter glue with 1 tablespoon liquid laundry detergent (any old kind will do). Use a spatula to mix well, adding more detergent as needed until the mixture no longer sticks to the sides of the bowl. Once the slime is ready, you can begin to stretch it, make shapes, or form glittery stick people. This solution doesn't stain when it comes in contact with surfaces, so don't worry about messing up your table or kitchen counter. Keep the slime stored at room temperature so you can break this out the next time the kids are bored.

○ CREATE A COLLAGE

Turn your old magazines and newspapers into a creative art project for all ages when your kids need something to keep them busy. From magazines to newspapers, you can find everything you need at home to create a collage that is fridge-worthy. Gather some scissors, paper or poster board, glue or tape, and old magazines to get started. With your kids' input, determine a theme for the collage and ask them to start hunting for appropriate pictures. For example, you can ask them to find funny faces or toys they want for their next birthday while sifting through magazines. Have them cut out their favorite images and then tape or glue them to a piece of construction paper or poster board to put on display. Older children can add funny captions to each picture in the collage to make this activity even more creative.

○ START A POETRY CLUB

When you have a houseful of children looking for something to do, prompt them to start a poetry club. Scour through books of poetry from the local library or find examples of limericks, haikus, or rhymes in your own book collection. Older children can also pull examples from their textbooks for inspiration. Once they have chosen their favorite type of poetry, ask them to brainstorm a topic and start writing. When the poems are ready, host a reading in your home. Ask each child to read his finished piece aloud and discuss his inspiration for the poem. From poems about family pets to poems about objects in your home, your child can express his creativity in his own way and share it with his friends. Make this activity a regular one by having the group create a name for their club and set up dates and times to meet regularly to read through their poetry.

○ MAKE A COMIC STRIP

No matter how old your child is, she has life experiences that can easily inspire illustrations. Gather paper, pens, pencils, and markers so she can turn her life story into a comic strip. Begin by showing your children examples of comic strips from newspapers. After the giggles subside, have your children brainstorm some of their favorite memories and experiences. Once they have chosen an event or memory to draw, help them sketch out a set of squares on a page, giving them space to draw each sequence leading up to the event. Add bubbles for text so they can accurately capture the experience. Once the comic strips are drawn, encourage your children to add bursts of color to the illustration with markers or crayons. Host a final reveal once the comic strips are complete so they can share their creativity.

○ SURPRISE A SIBLING

While small acts of kindness toward strangers is often the norm, you can show your kids how to value their siblings too. Start by sitting down with your children individually to discuss ways they can assist and surprise a sibling. For example, your older child can vacuum your younger child's room or pick up toys in the playroom, while a younger child can sneak into an older sibling's bedroom and make the bed. Have your kids secretly put together goody bags for each other to enjoy at snacktime. During the school year, siblings can also put kind notes in each other's lunch boxes to show they care. While the kind gestures may not squash *all* sibling squabbles, these acts can teach your children how kind gestures can brighten their days.

○ TELL A GROUP STORY

Turn those fits of boredom into fits of giggles with a group story session where each child gets to add his or her special touch to the plot line. Begin by brainstorming a topic for the group story and have your children decide on a title. You can start off the creative session with one line, such as "It was a dark and stormy night" or "One day, Peppy decided to go on an adventure." Have your children and their friends sit in a circle and take turns letting each child add one line to the story until everyone gets a turn. Designate one person to write down the story as you go along. Once each child has added a line to the story, add a plot twist that brings some excitement to the narrative, such as "But she didn't know what was coming" or "Her day took a turn for the worst when…" As the story unfolds, watch as the fun in your home evolves with each new line.

○ CREATE A FILL-IN-THE-BLANK BOOK

You don't have to spend time at the store or money on entertainment when your kids can create their very own Mad Libs book at home. As an added bonus, this activity helps teach your older children how to differentiate nouns, adverbs, verbs, and adjectives. Begin by gathering some blank pieces of paper and asking your children to choose a topic. Topics may range from a day at the beach to a school-day adventure. Ask each child to write out a sentence that pertains to the title and then write the story, leaving blank spots to customize the story later. Draw a line to replace nouns, descriptive words, and action words that can be filled in later. Once the story is complete, have your children take turns filling in new words that are silly to make the story unique and hilarious.

○ WRITE A TV SHOW SCRIPT

The entertainment doesn't have to stop when the TV is off. In fact, your children can tap into their creative minds to write an episode of their favorite show. This activity works especially well with a group of friends. Ask the children to decide which character each child will play. Select one child to write down the details for the opening scene and then have each character add dialogue to the script that models what normally happens on the TV show. For example, if one child is playing the adventurous character, have him or her brainstorm an activity that character could theoretically do. Encourage the group to discuss how the characters will interact with one another. Don't forget to add in a plot twist or an adventure that is humorous or silly. Once the script is done, find clothing and props to act out the scene or even move the furniture in your home to set up one of the scenes on the TV show. Stage a performance for the family or neighborhood parents and watch the script come to life.

○ ENJOY FLASHLIGHT GHOST STORIES

AGES 8-12

Turn a dull evening into a silly and scary experience with flashlight ghost stories. Break out some flashlights, find a comfy spot to sit, and gather for some spooky storytelling with the lights off. Get your kids' creative juices going by asking them to think about what makes their skin crawl, such as the sight of a spider or a scary monster hiding in the closet. Then, prompt each person to tell a ghost story while holding a flashlight pointing upward under his or her chin. Topics can include a scene in a dark forest or a ghost living in an old house, haunting all who visit. Add some creativity to the storytelling session by making shadow puppets on the wall while explaining what is happening as the characters travel through adventures. Although this activity is entertaining for older children, it may not be appropriate for little ones who are prone to nightmares.

○ WRITE NEW LYRICS TO FAVORITE MELODIES

AGES 6-12

You don't have to have a recording studio in your home to spur a jam session. Your kids can express their creativity and musical talent without even using instruments if they write new lyrics to their favorite melodies. Begin this activity by having each child write down the title of his or her favorite tune. Although they may know the words by heart, ask them to write new lyrics that flow with the melody. For example, if your little one loves "The Wheels on the Bus," use that melody to come up with a song about cupcakes, such as "The cupcakes Mommy makes are very good, very good, very good." Once the song is written, all that is left to do is perform the new jam. Older children may even want to add some dance moves and choreography to add another level of fun to this activity.

○ SEND A FAN LETTER TO A MUSICIAN

If your child has all the latest songs from her favorite band or singer on her playlist, make good use of screen-free time by helping her write a fan letter expressing her appreciation. Research the artist's address for fan mail and supply your swooning tween with stationery or blank paper and a pen to start writing. You can help her find just the right words to include by asking her what she likes most about the artist's songs, dance moves, or videos. Once the letter is complete, show her how to include a return address and place a stamp on the envelope before putting it in the mailbox. In some cases, musicians send autographed photos or letters back within a few weeks or months.

○ MAKE GLASS BOTTLE MUSIC

After a refreshing beverage on a hot summer day, turn those glass soda or juice bottles into an instrument that will entertain your kids. Simply gather several bottles together on a table and get your musicians ready to experiment. Each child can start by blowing into or over the top of an empty bottle to see what sound and tone it makes. Or, you can add a wooden spatula to the instrument collection to gently tap on the outside or rim of each bottle. Create various sounds by filling a few of the bottles with water. Your kids can evaluate how to make different tones by using a small amount of liquid in the bottle compared to a full bottle. Bring out their musical talents by trying to reproduce their favorite tunes or by having a sing-along with their homemade instruments.

○ CREATE MUSIC SHAKERS

AGES 6-8

Do your kids love those egg-shaped music shakers? Help them make their own with items you have lying around the house. All you need is a toilet paper roll, a tiny cardboard box, or a paper towel roll to get started. Simply staple, tape, or glue one end closed and fill with uncooked rice, nuts, or corn kernels. Secure the other end of the cardboard and get shaking. Encourage your kids to personalize their new music shakers by decorating the outside of the cardboard tube. Add swatches of tissue paper or colored construction paper with glue, or break out the crayons and markers so your children can write their names on the outside of the shaker. Once all the shakers are complete, let the musical performance begin.

○ MAKE BUSINESS CARDS

AGES 6-12

It's never too early to start thinking about the future, and this activity is designed to help your child think about his or her potential career—whether it's realistic or just silly. Show your kids a few sample cards, either your own or from another business. In order to keep the smiles and giggles abundant, encourage your younger kids to create funny business names. Brainstorm ideas such as "Sam's Smelly Office" or "Jenny's Jingling Jewelry" before breaking out construction paper, kid-friendly scissors, crayons, and markers. Then, cut pieces of construction paper or cardstock paper into small rectangular shapes, modeling the size of an average business card. Have your kids create logos and slogans to display on their business cards, along with fake phone numbers. Older kids might want to make something more realistic based on their interests. If you have a laminator, make these cards look more official with a clear coating.

◯ CHOREOGRAPH A NEW DANCE

AGES 6-12

Get shaking and moving when boredom sets in on those rainy days. Help your children choreograph a dance that combines legwork and arm movements from their favorite dancers or artists. Have each child come up with a choreographed dance and then have them merge their moves. Or, teach them some of your favorite dance moves in an informal way. Get creative by combining popular dances from different eras—for example, a Charleston step, the lawn mower, the sprinkler, or even jumping jacks. From slow dances to hip-hop movements that will leave the little ones breathless, your kids can do this any season of the year. Once the dance is ready to perform, gather an audience of friends and families to watch the show.

◯ PLAY NAME THAT TUNE

AGES 8-12

Put the electronics away and launch a game of Name That Tune to test your kids' musical abilities. You don't need a music player or iTunes to play a game that tests your knowledge of popular music from the present or the past—just hum the tunes yourself. Simply gather your children in a circle and make a list of songs on pieces of paper cut into strips. Once the family is ready to play, toss all the song titles on the paper strips into a bucket or hat. One by one, have each player choose a song from the hat or bucket and hum the melody. Set the rules for the game first to avoid any sibling squabbles. You can designate a particular partner to guess the song or open it up to the entire group. If you want, make the game more competitive by forming teams and tallying points for each correct guess.

○ HOST A TALENT SHOW

Do your kids like televised talent shows? Host one in your own home! Open the competition to friends, neighbors, and family members or host a sibling sing-off. Allow each participant to choose the talent he or she wants to showcase and give each person time to rehearse. Your child may want to sing his favorite song, highlight her soccer ball juggling skills, or use homemade instruments to play a song she just composed. Regardless of the talent, make this activity more impressive by writing down a lineup of performers and putting together a makeshift stage in the garage or outdoor patio for the final performance. You can even make homemade ribbons or trophies to award to the finalists. If you don't want to be the judge, ask grandparents or neighbors to sit in for the showcase event.

○ CRAFT TOOTHPICK STICK PEOPLE

AGES 6–10

Place a paper towel on a flat surface and have your kids arrange a few toothpicks in the shapes of stick people. Mix and match colored toothpicks if you have them to add a little variety to the activity. Once the toothpicks are arranged to your children's liking, add dabs of glue at the joints to piece them together. If you'd like to make larger stick people, use ice pop sticks instead. When the glue dries, your children can (gently) send these stick people on adventures throughout your home. Be careful, though, because the constructions may be fragile.

○ MAKE BOTTLE CAP ART

If your kids have been saving bottle caps and want to put them to good use, make bottle cap art. Begin by placing a piece of poster board or cardboard on a flat surface. Then, arrange the bottle caps into shapes. For example, you and your children can make a large heart. Your little artists can also personalize each creation. Break out acrylic paints and paintbrushes to add bursts of color to the caps. Apply stickers or even glitter with a dab of glue on the caps for a sparkling effect. Once the decorating work is complete, glue each cap onto the poster board or cardboard in the shapes your kids created. From a green and brown turtle arrangement to a bright yellow star, the options for bottle cap art are endless.

○ CUT PAPER SNOWFLAKES

When snow is falling outside but it's too cold to build a snowman, make your own winter wonderland inside your home. All you need is a white piece of 8½" x 11" paper and a few pairs of kid-safe scissors to get started. Begin with a rectangular piece of white paper and fold the paper diagonally to form a triangle shape. Continue by folding the triangle shape into three separate sections vertically. Then, let the cutting begin. The kids can form various shapes by cutting off portions of the triangle. Get creative and let your children make as many cuts as they would like. Once the cutting is complete, unfold the pieces. Tape or glue the snowflake shapes on a colored piece of paper or cardboard to display.

○ COLOR PAPER WINDOW CLINGS

Got clingy kids? Help them make window clings instead! Grab some contact paper to unleash their creativity and bring colorful artwork to your indoor and outdoor areas. All you need for this activity is some basic art supplies, such as markers or paints and paintbrushes and clear or white contact paper. Start off by cutting the contact paper into just the right size for your child's artwork. Then, let her decorate the paper to her heart's desire with markers or paints or even a combination of the two. Have your children draw a row of blooming flowers or funny faces. Or, you can choose a theme, such as superheroes or cartoon characters. Once the drawings are complete, cut out the shapes to eliminate any excess white paper around the art. Peel off the backing on the contact paper and stick the artwork to windows all around your home.

○ MAKE WAX PAPER PLACEMATS

Kids won't mind setting the dinner table when they can grab placemats they created! To get started with this activity, cut off two rectangular-shaped sheets of wax paper for each child. Make sure the sheets are big enough to hold a plate and silverware. Place a sheet on top of a large brown paper bag and tape it down to a table or other flat surface. Let your children decorate the wax paper however they like. They can use crayons to draw on it or place pieces of construction paper in various shapes on the wax paper. Once the design is ready, place a clean piece of wax paper over the decorated piece of wax paper. Top that with another large brown paper bag and iron over the top to melt the design into the wax paper. (Make sure that Mom or Dad helps out with the ironing.) Once the wax paper has cooled, simply place your new placemats on the table and get ready to dine in style.

○ CRAFT SHOE BOX TRAINS

If your little engineer needs a few more choo-choos for his collection, you don't have to run to the store to buy the latest toy. Instead, make homemade trains using empty shoe boxes. With a few sheets of construction paper, some kid-safe scissors, and a dab of glue, you can transform those shoe boxes into a locomotive your little one will treasure. Begin by brainstorming how your children want to decorate their new train. Sift through sheets of construction paper to find just the right colors for the base of the train and the wheels. Cut strips of paper to cover the sides of the shoe box and glue or tape the paper before cutting circles to place the wheels on the side of the train. Get creative when decorating by using stickers or plastic wrap to make windows. Once the boxes are fully decorated, attach them to one another by poking holes in the end of each box and stringing them together with yarn or fishing line. The only thing left to do is take the train on an excursion.

○ PRODUCE AN IMPROMPTU PLAY

It's no secret that your children have wild imaginations. Let them put their never-ending stories and plot twists to good use with an impromptu play in your living room or backyard. Make a list of characters for the play and assign each child a part. Then, ask your children to come up with a scene for the play and a plot, complete with a dramatic twist toward the end. Once the play script is in place, scour your home to find costumes appropriate for each part and even props to use to enhance the performance. Get ready for showtime and watch the drama unfold before your eyes as your kids put the play into action for the family, neighbors, or friends.

○ PLAY DRESS-UP

No matter what style of clothes the adults in your house wear, chances are good that your kids want to try on those outfits. A game of dress-up is an easy option for those days when your kids need some entertainment. While you sort through old clothes, pull out a few shirts, pants, dresses, hats, or ties and let your kids giggle while picking through their favorites. Have each child mix and match crazy clothing and add old jewelry, headbands, and scarves to each outfit. If you have some old shoes, watch as your young ones clomp around in Dad's boots or Mom's heels. Make this activity quite the production with a fashion show to showcase the creative outfits your children put together.

○ CRAFT A CEREAL NECKLACE

Circular cereal is a staple in almost every home with young kids. Grab a handful and turn it into a necklace. This simple activity can help younger kids with finger dexterity, learning patterns, and measuring. Gather a variety of styles of cereal with ready-made holes, such as Cheerios or Froot Loops, and line up the cereal on a table or work station. Cut a piece of yarn that will fit around your child's neck very loosely and have your little one begin stringing the yarn through the pieces of cereal. Tie the ends of the yarn together once all the cereal is placed on the necklace. The best part? She has a snack ready if she gets hungry!

○ MAKE PAPER PLATE MASKS

Have a handful of paper plates left over from a party or picnic? Let your kids get artsy and transform them into masks. It doesn't matter if you have plain white paper plates or plates with designs or borders; your child can personalize these plates and create his or her new persona for the day. Cut holes for the eyes, nose, and mouth, and then gather crayons, construction paper, acrylic paints, watercolor paints, and markers. Then the kids can begin making masks that resemble anything they want—a fairy, a superhero, an animal, or even a scary face. Attach a piece of yarn or string with glue to each side of the plate to create a headband that offers a perfect fit.

○ PLAY BLINDFOLD GUIDES

When those sibling squabbles have reached a breaking point, teach your children how to work together with this trust-based—but fun!—activity. Using a ready-made blindfold or even a light scarf or bandana, you can launch an activity that helps build stronger bonds between siblings or friends. The object of this activity is to let one participant serve as the "eyes" for the other player. Designate a route the players must take—either inside or outside. Start by putting the blindfold on one child. Let the other child gently guide him through the path. The children must communicate with each other and properly guide each other to avoid injury. For example, instruct your kids to point out any furniture in the way or steps the child must navigate. The child serving as the "eyes" is also responsible for describing objects along the path to help guide the player.

○ MAKE COTTON BALL SNOWMEN

Bring a chill into your home without the harsh wind of a snowstorm when helping your kids make cotton ball snowmen. With a piece of construction paper, a dab of glue, and various sizes of cotton balls, watch as winter consumes your household with this fun activity. Simply gather the cotton balls in a pile and have your children pick through them to find the perfect size for their snowman. Arrange the bigger cotton balls at the base of the snowman and use smaller cotton balls for the middle part of the body and the head of the snowman. On the construction paper, draw a large circle of glue for the base, a medium-sized circle for the body, and a smaller circle for the head. Fill in the circles with glue and begin attaching the cotton balls. Add a bit of character and color to each snowman by using raisins for eyes, orange paper for the nose, and black paper cut into small circles for the buttons.

○ CREATE YOUR OWN NURSERY RHYMES

Lots of children love to sing common nursery rhymes. Take that interest to the next level by having them create their own nursery rhymes. It may be difficult for younger children to think of their own words and rhymes, so start off the nursery rhyme with a common phrase, such as "Jack and Jill went up the hill to…" Then the kids can add their own words to finish the phrase, such as "to meet their mommy and daddy." This activity doesn't have to be a solo act, though. Invite siblings and friends over to bust out some rhymes collaboratively. With more creative minds in the mix, there's no telling how unique each nursery rhyme can be.

○ PAINT CLOWN FACES

You don't have to have specialized paint or big red rubber noses to transform your kids into clowns when they feel like being a little silly. All you need is a little makeup to get the giggles going. With the help of an adult, add bright colors to their faces to prepare for an in-home circus. Begin by putting brightly colored eye shadow on your children's eyelids using a makeup brush. Give them a tube of bright red lipstick and let them draw round circles on their cheeks to showcase their rosy spirits. Use an eyeliner stick to draw shapes or lines down their noses or to accent the creases in their foreheads for added effect. Once the clown transformation is complete, complement the look by encouraging your kids to dress in bright clothing and perform an impromptu circus for the family.

○ PLAY "MOM" AND "DAD"

It's common for your little ones to mimic your behavior; however, with this activity, they can take the imitation to a professional level. Ask each child to brainstorm what Mommy and Daddy do on a typical day, both at home and work, and then let the mimicking begin. You may need some props for this activity. For instance, if Mommy carries a work bag on her way out the door, have your little executive grab a bag from the closet to carry. If Daddy is a teacher, see if your son or daughter can teach a lesson to his or her siblings. See just how creative your kids can be with accessories and play-acting. Write down the phrases they say and snap a few pictures as they re-enact the lives of Mom and Dad for the day.

◯ MAKE SHAVING CREAM ART

AGES 8–12

Prepare for a messy, yet fun, day when breaking out cans of shaving cream for this activity. Simply lay down a tarp or sheet on the floor or sidewalk to capture any leftover messes. While your children can create art by spraying shaving cream directly on the grass or sidewalk, you can also provide them with colored poster board or cardboard boxes to practice their skills. Lay down the cardboard or poster board on the tarp or sheet and then let them spray onto them directly from the can. Add a bit of color to their artwork by putting some shaving cream into a bowl and adding food coloring so they can use paintbrushes to decorate the poster boards. Before letting their creativity go wild, instruct them how to carefully spray the shaving cream, and make sure they are wearing protective glasses or spraying away from others to avoid any soapy cream entering their eyes.

◯ MAKE A PAPER TETRIS BOARD GAME

AGES 8–12

You don't need electronics to play one of your favorite computer games. Instead, create your own Tetris-like board game using construction paper and poster board. Begin by having your kids cut colored pieces of construction paper into various shapes. For example, cut squares, rectangles, and L-shaped wedges. Next, draw a grid on a large piece of white poster board to use as your game board. Once you are ready to play, take turns placing each shape on the board while trying to leave as few white spaces as possible. You can add an element of surprise to the game by putting all the cut shapes into a brown paper bag and having each child randomly draw a game piece when it is his or her turn. Form teams or play individually—whichever works best for your crowd.

○ BECOME A HUMAN MUMMY

When your children need a chance to break the rules and get a little silly, this activity is perfect. Grab a few rolls of toilet paper and head into the living room or outdoors to transform each child into a human mummy. It's simple to have your kids wrap each other up in toilet paper, but you may need some duct tape or clips to secure their new costumes. When you have all the supplies ready, let them roll the toilet paper around each other. Tuck in their arms by wrapping the TP around the entire body and leave holes for the mouth, nose, and eyes. Challenge your children to make their mummy costumes unique. For example, one may choose to wrap only his legs while another child may choose to wrap her entire body. Once the toilet paper is secure, let the mummy walks begin.

○ HAVE HAIR SALON FUN

Offer your kids and their friends a bit of pampering with this screen-free activity. Pretend you are all going to the hair salon and prepare the supplies for the visit. You will need brushes, combs, clips, rubber bands, hairspray, and bobby pins to perfect various cool styles. Have the children pair off and decide who will be the stylist and who will be the client, and then help them decide on hairstyles—anything from ponytails and braids to buns or Mohawks. When using straight irons or curling irons and products such as hairspray, gel, or mousse, make sure an adult is present to supervise. Once the hairstyles are complete, take this activity to a glamorous level by putting on dress-up clothes to strut down an imaginary runway.

○ CRAFT HOMEMADE CLAY

Get crafty in the kitchen by helping your kids make their very own Play-Doh–like clay, providing them with material to mold and mush whenever boredom sets in. With just a couple of inexpensive ingredients you can whip up a batch of modeling clay in no time. Start by scooping 2 tablespoons of cornstarch into a medium-sized mixing bowl. Add 3 squirts tempera paint in the color of your choice and begin mixing until you have a thick paste. Continue to knead and mix to achieve the desired consistency. If your modeling clay is too wet, add more cornstarch; if it is too dry, add more paint. Repeat the process with different colors of paint to create modeling clay in every color of the rainbow.

○ CREATE ICE POP STICK ART

Ice pops are a favorite summertime treat for kids of all ages. Once the sweet treat has been consumed, save those sticks for a screen-free art project to keep your kids busy. (You can also purchase a box of ice pop sticks from a local craft store to get ready for a day of art.) When making ice pop stick art, you and the kids have plenty of options for colorful masterpieces. Glue the sticks together vertically or horizontally and offer your kids a blank canvas to paint or color with markers. Or, glue the sticks together into different shapes. For example, you could arrange four sticks into an open square, secure them with glue, and use the final product as a photo frame. Have some markers, paints, and paintbrushes on hand so your kids can personalize the sticks.

⃝ MAKE TISSUE BUTTERFLIES

Your home likely has a box (or a few boxes) of tissues lying around. Why not use these tissues for a creative art project when your kids are restless? All you need is a few pipe cleaners and tissues to transform tissues (or paper coffee filters, if you have any) into beautiful butterflies. Line up your pipe cleaners and gather one tissue for each child. On a piece of paper, have each child trace the shape of a butterfly and then secure the tissue underneath the paper before cutting out the sketch. You can also cinch the tissue in the middle if cutting proves to be too difficult for little ones. Next, fold each pipe cleaner in half and tuck two of the cut pieces of tissue into the fold of the pipe cleaner. Twist the top of the pipe cleaner to form an antenna to finish the project. If your children want to add a little sparkle to their new creations, consider gluing sequins or glitter to the tissues before attaching them to the pipe cleaners.

⃝ PLAY OBJECT HIDE-AND-SEEK

Put a new twist on hide-and-seek by using small items or toys in your home for hunting. Ideal for both indoor and outdoor play, this activity gives your children a reason to search high and low. Simply choose a few small items in your home, such as a toy, trinket, plastic ball, or even tiny pieces of candy (if you hide food, just be sure you know where the kids put it!). Assign one child to go and hide the treasures. Encourage your child to get creative and hide the items in hard-to-find places. The options are endless for this game. Once the hiding is complete, allow the rest of your kids to seek to see who can find the most objects. Take turns assigning hiders and seekers to keep this activity going all day long.

○ GO PANTRY SHOPPING

AGES 6–12

Even though you may get annoyed when your kids stand in the kitchen complaining that there is "nothing to eat," that sentiment is the inspiration for this activity. Send your kids to the "store" without actually leaving the house when pantry shopping. Prepare your budding shoppers for a fun-filled math lesson that combines food and cash. Simply gather some play money from an old board game or use real change and supply each child with a budget for the shopping trip. Label the food in the pantry with prices using stickers or strips of paper taped to the boxes and canned goods. Grab reusable grocery bags to help them gather up their selections. Once a shopper is determined and a checker is chosen, send your kids straight to the pantry to spend their "money." The checker adds up the items while placing the groceries in bags. Make this activity even more interesting by seeing if your children can buy ingredients for an actual meal or side dish.

○ DYE EGGS

AGES 6–12

Although most people reserve dyeing eggs for the spring season, why not do it any time of the year? Have an adult put eggs and water in a saucepan and boil on the stove. Once boiling, turn off the stove and let the eggs stand for about ten minutes before putting the eggs in a strainer. Once the eggs are completely cooled, place bowls on a table and add ½ cup boiling water, 1 teaspoon vinegar, and about 10 drops food coloring to each. Dip each egg into the cups of dye for a few minutes and set aside to dry. (If you want to keep the mess isolated, consider using an outdoor area.)

○ DRAW A FAMILY TREE

Teach your kids about their heritage and family members with this family-friendly activity. All you need is a large piece of paper or poster board, a few markers or crayons, and knowledge of your family history. Begin by sitting down with your children and looking through old family photo albums or scrapbooks. Have your children write down the names of each person they know or can remember meeting. Next, draw a large tree on the poster board or paper and create branches stemming from the base. Start by listing grandparents at the top of the tree with Mom's grandparents on the right and Dad's on the left. List each child of the grandparents and then include Mom's and Dad's names underneath their parents' names. Have your children write their names at the base of the tree. If you need a little help remembering names, give an older relative a call to verify. Display the final result at your next family gathering.

○ MAKE A BABY-THEMED SCRAPBOOK

As your kids get older, they may not remember just how cute they were when they were barely walking. Make these memories fresh in their minds by prompting them to create a scrapbook of their baby pictures. Scour through old photos or have some printed before you begin this activity. Ask each child to choose his or her favorite pics and begin gluing or taping each one on colored construction paper. Beyond that, you can get as creative as you want. Cut pictures into shapes, add stickers or photo corners, or add extras such as a hospital bracelet. Once the pages are decorated, punch holes in each page and string yarn through the holes to bind the scrapbook. Keep these books in a safe place so you can break them out for pure entertainment when your kids' friends are visiting.

○ DESIGN DENIM JOURNALS

Whether or not it's back-to-school time, you can keep the kids occupied and away from electronics while also reusing old jeans! Choose notebooks to use for school or as journals for your children and get to decorating them with denim. Have the kids help you cut up an old pair of jeans into squares. Using glue or a glue gun, help your children create a collage of denim on the fronts of the notebooks. Place squares of denim in a variety of patterns and if your kids want a splash of color, mix in a few solid-colored pieces of fabric or felt to the designs. Make the backs of the notebooks just as decorative with a few squares of denim in a similar design.

○ TOP THE POPCORN

When your crew is hungry for some popcorn, this activity is the ideal way to make snacktime much more interesting. The goal is to challenge your kids to try new flavors and spices to open their minds to eating new things. Help them pop some popcorn in the microwave and then pour just a little bit of popcorn into several bowls lined up on a table. Next, ask your children to look through the pantry or your spice cabinet to find just the right topping for their bowls. From cinnamon and sugar to garlic salt or chili powder, you may be surprised by the concoctions your children come up with during this activity. When the spices and flavors have been added, each child gets a chance to try a bite out of each bowl.

○ HAVE DESSERT IN THE BATHTUB

Put a fun twist on bath time and eliminate the mess from indoor ice pop eating with this activity for your little ones who crave sweet treats. All you need is a bathtub full of water and a few ice pops. Although your kids may think you're crazy for suggesting dessert in the bathtub, it's the perfect way to give them an after-dinner treat and get them ready to clean up the dirt and grime that results from a productive day outside. Have your kids put on their swimsuits and toss in a few bath toys before handing them ice pops. Let them pick a color or make it a game to see who can guess the color of the ice pop hiding behind your back before letting them dive into the sticky dessert. Then, break out the soap and start bath time.

○ DECORATE YOUR SKIN

Let your little ones express their individuality and creativity with an activity that gets super sticky, yet colorful. If you have stickers lying around or body paint, opt for this outdoor activity instead of a day in front of the TV. The object of this activity is to decorate your skin in ways that showcase creativity. Ask your children to choose a few stickers to stick on their legs and arms while outside or break out the body paint while at the beach and let them draw designs on each other's arms and legs. Parents willing to take this activity to a semipermanent level can add washable tattoos to the activity, but know that it may take a few days for these pieces of art to wash off. Once the body art is complete, have your children do a runway walk or parade around outside to show off their body art. Then, break out the hose or have the kids jump into the water to wash off their body art.

○ CREATE A CHAIR PLAYMATE

Turn a functional piece of furniture into a playmate for your children if they're looking for company. With just a few kitchen chairs, you can bring your furniture to life and giggle for the rest of the afternoon while admiring your chair people. Explain to the kids that the goal is to dress up the chairs to look like people. Have your children bring a few articles of clothing from their closets and dresser drawers to your kitchen. Lay out pants on the seat of each chair and then put a shirt over the back of each chair. Add a pair of shoes on the floor. You can even hook a pair of socks from the pants and droop them into the shoes for a more realistic look. Once the headless chairs are dressed, make faces on construction paper to tape to the back of each chair.

○ CELEBRATE THE WRONG HOLIDAY

Keep the holiday spirit alive and thriving in your home regardless of the time of year by launching this activity, which calls for celebrating a holiday at the wrong time of the year. Whether you choose to celebrate Hanukkah in July, Halloween in March, or Valentine's Day in November, the festivities are bound to keep your children entertained. Start by determining which holiday you and the kids want to celebrate. For younger children, this is a great opportunity to teach them more about the traditions and timing of holidays throughout the year. Once you've determined the holiday, start combing through your home for decorations. For instance, you can create spooky signs on black construction paper using white chalk or hang red streamers throughout the house for a heart-filled celebration. Teach the kids about giving to each other by celebrating Christmas or Hanukkah, complete with self-wrapped presents they have gathered from their rooms and are willing to part with to gift to a sibling. Make traditional cookies or snacks to coordinate with your festive day too.

○ CREATE AUTOGRAPHED CLOTHING ■□□

Show your kids that they are rock stars by staging an autograph session when their friends are over. As a bonus: use this activity to help them clean out their closets to find old T-shirts or jackets to decorate and autograph. Once your children have chosen an old T-shirt that offers room for signatures and decorations, gather up their friends and host a signing party. Using fabric markers or even permanent markers, allow each kid to write a message on the clothing. Phrases such as "friends forever" and "you are my sunshine" will give your child's self-esteem a boost and his or her clothing a decorative, personalized look. Make the autographs permanent by outlining each phrase, illustration, or signature with fabric paint before letting the ink dry. Once the signatures are complete, have each child model the signed clothing. Make sure you hand-wash the clothing to keep the memorable messages vibrant. You can also soak the clothing in vinegar before washing to ensure that the ink sets.

○ CRAFT VEGGIE DOLLS ■■□

Turn ordinary vegetables into friendly playmates with this activity. Even if your kids don't like eating the corn or cucumbers on their plates, they may change their tune once they make friends with these veggies. To make veggie dolls, start by stocking up on corn on the cob, celery, cucumbers, asparagus, or even tomatoes. Remove the husks from the corn, stems from the tomatoes, and clean each vegetable. Each child can choose a veggie to decorate into his or her own doll. Next, break out some markers to personalize the vegetables. Have your children draw eyes, noses, and mouths right on the vegetables. Create hair by helping your kids glue strands of yarn to the head of each veggie. Set out each veggie doll for others to see and then serve your children the remainder of the undecorated veggies as a snack.

○ MAKE A KEEPSAKE TREASURE BOX

■□□

All of your kids probably have items that they hold close and dear. Whether it is a small blanket, a rock, a baseball card, or a card from a relative, they need a place to store these treasures. With this activity, you and your kids can build a treasure box for all of these mementos using household items. First, find just the right structure for each child's treasure box. It could be a shoe box or a shipping box or a plastic container with a lid. Next, brainstorm ways to decorate each treasure box. For example, one child may want to draw pictures on a white piece of paper and glue the paper on the box, while another child may want to add stickers to the exterior of a plastic container and draw shapes with a magic marker. Make sure to add each child's name to the top of the box and explain that these boxes are personal and only the owner can view them or add items.

○ MAKE EGG PEOPLE

■■■

Turn ordinary eggshells into plant people with this activity designed for the green thumbs in your family. Due to the delicate nature of eggshells, it may be best for Mom or Dad to do some preparation beforehand. Delicately hold each egg over the sink and poke a hole in the bottom with a pin. Next, cut off the top quarter of the eggshell with small scissors. Empty the yolk and gently rinse out the eggshells. Next, let each child draw a face and hair on the eggshells with markers. Then, fill each egg with soil and grass seed and place the eggs into an empty egg carton. Each day, have your children water the eggs and monitor the growth of the grass seeds to see which "person" matures first.

○ HOST RAINBOW WARS

Add a little color to those dreary, rainy days by hosting a rainbow war activity in the kitchen. Arm your kids with aprons and play clothes and then prepare to "wow" them with a rainbow of colors. For this activity, you will need glass jars or bowls and various colors of food coloring. Once the aprons are securely tied and your kids are ready to go, put some newspaper or an old tablecloth on your workspace. Fill up each glass jar halfway with water. Next, line up one bottle of food coloring next to each jar of water. Then, have each child choose a color and very carefully add a drop of food coloring into his or her jar. After they watch the water transform, have your children move along to the next glass jar, taking along their food coloring to add a drop into each jar to create a rainbow of colors. Talk about the various colors that evolve as the colors are combined during this activity. For example, red and yellow make orange, and blue and yellow combinations make green.

○ GUESS THE WEIGHTS

When the kids are bored, grab an unusual household item to entertain them: your bathroom scale! Bring the scale into your kitchen or an area of your home with hardwood floor or tile and begin a game of Guess the Weight. Even if your scale is typically used to weigh people, it will probably work for other objects as well. For instance, your kids could weigh a schoolbook, remote-control car, or box of wooden blocks. Before placing any items on the scale, have each child guess how much the object weighs. Write down the estimates and then reveal the correct answer by placing the item on the scale. The child whose guess is closest to the actual weight wins that round.

○ CRAFT SOAP SCULPTURES

You don't need to enroll your children in a ceramics class to create sculptures when you can use a bar of soap to spark their creativity. Crafting soap sculptures encourages clean fun, but since using a small knife is required, this activity is best for tweens. Place a bar of soap in front of each child at your kitchen or dining room table. Then, give each of them a small, dull knife such as a butter knife or plastic knife to begin shaping the soap. Discuss shapes they can carve such as a heart or a turtle by shaving off parts of the soap with the knife. Your children may also want to etch out messages or inscribe their name in the soap sculpture. Minimize the mess by placing a paper towel underneath each bar of soap to catch the shavings.

○ DESIGN A SHAPE-BASED FABRIC COLLAGE

If your kids are tired of coloring, give them a colorful project that uses fabric instead of paper. With a large piece of poster board or cardboard as the platform, get ready to see their creativity come to life with a fabric collage that uses different shapes to make bigger pictures. Supply each child with glue and kid-friendly scissors. Then, sort through different remnants of fabric you have at home. You can also cut up old T-shirts or clothing for this activity. Have each child cut different shapes to glue onto the cardboard platform—for example, a big circle and small triangles to make a sun and its rays. Or, opt for a uniform look with perfectly cut squares to arrange into a colorful pattern. Organize the layout of the collage before adding glue to the back of the fabric pieces. Firmly press each piece of fabric to the platform to secure the collage. Then, step back and admire the masterpiece.

○ DRAW A COLLABORATIVE MURAL

If you have a large group of kids who are bored, try this fun art project. This activity works best if you have a large roll of paper. However, you can also piece together regular sheets of paper with tape or glue to create a large canvas. Line the paper on a long dining room table or the floor. Next, determine the theme for the mural, such as animals, people, a specific outdoor scene. Then, let the kids get to work by designating one section of the paper for each child. They can use crayons, markers, stickers, or even watercolors to bring the blank canvas to life. Display this masterpiece on a wall in your home.

○ MAKE PORTABLE BEAN BAGS

If your outdoor equipment and bouncy balls have seen better days, craft your very own bean bags to inspire some outdoor games. Start by having the kids cut out a few square pieces of fabric. You only need two squares for each bean bag. Use a glue gun to secure the bottom and sides of the fabric together (an adult should handle this step). Once the fabric dries, the kids can fill the bags with rice, dry corn, or beans. Hot glue the top of the bag to secure it (again, children shouldn't handle a hot glue gun, so Mom or Dad will need to help them with this step). Repeat the process and create as many bags as you want before launching a bean bag toss game in the backyard.

○ PLAY HIDE THE TIMER

AGES 6-12
■□□

Hide-and-seek is often a go-to game when the kids are bored, but with a standard kitchen timer you can prompt all kids to seek without any hiders necessary. Before launching this game, designate one child as the person responsible for the timer. Show your kids how to set the timer. Then, set the timer for a designated time, such as two or three minutes, and send one child off to hide the timer somewhere in your home. Once hidden, unleash the seekers to find the timer. The object of the game is to find the timer before the buzzer rings. Take turns designating each child as the person who hides the timer until the fun of this activity has buzzed off.

○ WRITE INVISIBLE MESSAGES

AGES 6-12
■□□

Bring a little magic into an ordinary day with an activity that produces invisible messages. All you need is a dish, lemon juice, toothpicks, a flashlight, and a few pieces of paper to show your kids a magic trick that adds some mystery to the day. First, place a shallow dish filled with lemon juice on the table. Next, cut off the tip of a toothpick and dip one end of it into the lemon juice. Using the saturated toothpick, write out a message on the piece of paper. Let it dry. While the paper seems blank, the message will appear when you shine a flashlight on it. Surprise the kids with a message such as "Dessert is in the oven" or "It's snacktime" to get them even more excited about writing invisible messages.

○ CRAFT CRAYON CREATIONS

Take ordinary crayons and transform them into wonders you can hang throughout your home with this activity. Place a sheet of wax paper in front of each child on a table and dump out some broken and heavily used crayons. Have the kids begin unwrapping them. Then take a cheese grater and show your children how to make shavings from different crayons so that they have a rainbow of colored shavings on the piece of wax paper. As a precaution, have the kids wear gloves when using a cheese grater. Have your child arrange the shavings into a design, shape, or phrase. Then, place another piece of wax paper on top of the design and cover the entire creation with a sheet of newspaper. Next, heat up an iron and let your children watch as you gently run the warm iron over the newspaper for about ten seconds. Let the masterpiece dry and then peel back the newspaper and wax paper to reveal the final piece of art. Display their masterpieces by poking a small hole in the top of the shape and hanging it in your home.

○ TEST YOUR BACKWARD-WRITING SKILLS

Once they've got a really good handle on writing letters, let your kids experiment with writing backward. Besides pencil and paper, you will also need a small handheld mirror or access to a larger mirror for this activity. Start by asking each child to write a simple sentence backward. Something easy such as "I am a cat" is ideal to start with. Arm each child with a handheld mirror or have them take turns standing in front of a full-length mirror. Show them that the trick to writing backward is to look in the mirror to see the image of the paper when writing. Once the messages or phrases are written, hold up the paper to the mirror to see if the writing is legible.

○ MAKE COFFEE CAN STILTS

Does the smallest in your crew want to be taller, just like her older brothers or sisters? With this activity, your children can rise to a new level while testing their balance on homemade stilts. For this activity, you'll need empty coffee cans or large frozen juice cans to serve as the base of the stilts. While outside on the porch or in your garage, have your children step on each can to ensure they will hold their weight. If the test is successful, begin crafting the stilts by attaching a long piece of heavy rope or strong string to the sides of the cans with duct tape. The string or rope should stretch to the length of your child's legs so he or she can easily hold it while standing on the coffee cans. Once the stilts are crafted, let your kids try them out while walking outside. For safety purposes, it's best to have your kids wear a helmet and knee pads while walking on the stilts.

○ BUILD A CEREAL TOWER

Is your recycling bin overflowing with boxes? Your kids can build a magical tower with these boxes. (You can use full boxes as well if need be.) If the boxes are empty, your kids might want to wrap each one with white paper and decorate them with crayons, markers, or acrylic paint. Get creative by cutting out flaps for doors or windows on a few of the boxes for the tower. Once the designs have dried, it's time to start stacking. Show your kids how to balance the boxes—using full boxes for the bottom layer—and then layer each box to build an impressive structure.

○ MAKE AN ABC CHAIN

Have fun with the alphabet with just a few sheets of construction paper, kid-friendly scissors, and a large open space. Begin by cutting the construction paper into twenty-six squares. Next, have your children label each square with a letter of the alphabet (using lowercase or capital letters). Dark markers work best for this activity so each child can easily see the letter from a distance. Once all the squares are labeled, shuffle the papers and distribute an even amount to each child. Announce each letter of the alphabet and have the child with the appropriate letter begin the chain, starting with the letter *A*. Place each letter side by side, creating a winding road in the middle of your living room. Once you reach *Z*, shuffle again and repeat the process to create a new shape or chain.

○ CRAFT PERSONALIZED DOOR HANGERS

Help your children add a personal touch to their bedroom decor by crafting personalized door hangers. Start by gathering a piece of cardboard, cardstock paper, or a hefty box to serve as the base of the door hanger. Cut a rectangular piece with kid-friendly scissors and then create a circular hanger shape at the top to hang on a doorknob. Cover the cardboard with white or colored paper and let your kids decorate the door hanger. Encourage them to think of innovative phrases beyond "Do Not Disturb" to include on their personalized hangers. For example, sports fans may want "Cubs Fans Only" and avid readers could write "Book Worms Welcome!" Add some texture and color to the door hangers by attaching stickers, writing in glitter glue, or drawing illustrations in brightly colored markers.

○ PAINT DOT MASTERPIECES

Painting with dots imitates the famous pointillism paintings of Seurat, Van Gogh, and Pissarro. The object of this activity is to create kid-friendly designs, shapes, and illustrations using only dots instead of brushstrokes. Start by setting out cups of acrylic paint in different colors or even a set of watercolors. Give your children blank pieces of white paper and thin paintbrushes or cotton swabs and have them try to create shapes using only dots. Whether they choose to use large dots or small dots, they should ultimately make shapes with dots alone. If the paint gets too messy, try this activity with markers on construction paper.

○ CREATE A FAMILY LOGO

Find out how your kids envision your family's personality and legacy by challenging them to create a family logo together. With a little brainstorming about symbols, designs, or images that define your family, you can get your kids started on this collaborative activity. For example, if your family is brave, your logo could show a lion. After your children determine the design for the logo, supply them with the tools they need to make this logo a reality, such as crayons, markers, paper, or construction paper. Be sure each child adds an element to the design. (You could create a shield with four sections, then have each child decorate one-fourth of the logo with a symbol or illustration.) Once the logo is finished, proudly display it on your refrigerator or frame it to hang in your entryway for visitors to see.

○ DRAW PICTURES WITH FEET, NOT HANDS

Opt for a new twist on drawing when you get the kids' toes involved. With this activity, all you need is a piece of paper, crayons, and of course, a few toes to produce artwork and a few giggles. This challenge requires some concentration and some coordination, but kids will think it's hysterical. Simply lay down a piece of paper on a hard surface, such as hardwood floors or tile flooring. You can even use the garage or basement floor. Next, have each child nestle a crayon in between his or her toes and use it to draw a picture. Be sure to snap a few photos of the artistic expressions.

○ CRAFT A FOOD FACE

Magazines are overflowing with ads for food and restaurants. Make the advertisements useful by using these to craft a customized food face art piece. First, gather a few magazines for the kids to browse, then have them cut out food items using kid-friendly scissors. Next, they can construct a face on a blank piece of white paper. For example, a bushel of grapes may serve well as hair while a tomato may make the perfect nose. Glue or tape the food items to the piece of white paper. Once the creative food faces have dried, hang them up for all to admire. You can even add a competitive element to this activity by having each child secretly vote for the most creative food face.

○ MAKE MILK JUG PIGGY BANKS

If your kids want a little more spending money, launch a project that encourages them to save by making a piggy bank with common household items. All you need is a few empty milk jugs, some crafting materials, and a creative mind to put this activity into motion. Once you and the kids have thoroughly cleaned and dried empty milk cartons, cut a small slit in the top of the jug for your children; this will serve as the entry point for change or dollar bills. Next, have each child choose an animal. While many may want to stay true to the piggy bank name by drawing a pig, others may choose to have chicken banks or duck banks. Using construction paper, stickers, markers, and even acrylic paint, let your kids decorate their new banks. They can add duck feet by gluing orange construction paper to the bottom of the jug or even add bird wings to the sides with construction paper. Once the designs dry, set these banks in a designated spot and encourage your children to insert spare change or even a portion of their allowance.

○ MASTER MIMICKING MIRRORS

Take "follow the leader" to a creative level with a game of mimicking mirrors. Simply pair up your children to get started and to launch the laughter. The purpose of this game is to mimic your partner's actions, facial expressions, and movements. Start by designating one person as the leader and as the two sit and look at each other, the leader should make faces, hand gestures, or small movements that the follower must imitate. You can even allow them to speak, sing, or shout to make the activity more interesting and entertaining. Time the activity and then have the children switch roles. If you have several groups of children playing, stipulate that the first team to laugh is eliminated from that round to determine a winning duo.

○ BUILD AN INDOOR "SAND"BOX

If a rainy day has put a damper on your outdoor play plans, bring the fun inside with this activity. Create the structure for the sandbox by placing a large plastic tub in your living room. Next, add uncooked rice to the plastic tubs. When the tubs are full, let each kid get creative with his or her playtime, pouring the rice from one cup to another, or sifting it through a sieve. If you don't want to risk a mess inside, consider conducting this activity on a covered porch or garage area.

○ PLAY THE RULE GAME

While your children may be resistant to your rules, when *they* are calling the shots, they probably won't mind them! If you're having trouble getting them to follow rules in your home, this activity may be just what they need to think about rules differently. You don't need any supplies to get started—just a few creative minds. Begin by brainstorming the rules of the game, which can last for an hour or even the entire day. For instance, one child may determine that you must skip when entering the kitchen while another child may suggest that the word *no* is forbidden for a few hours. Let each child come up with a funny rule for the day and then create a score sheet to keep track of which kid violates the rules. At the end of a timed period or even the day, the child with the least amount of violations wins the game.

◯ PLAY THE SILENT GAME

When your house is a little too noisy for your liking, set the stage for some silence, and some fun. The silent game is often challenging, but it can prompt your children to get creative with their communication methods. The goal of the game is to refrain from talking for a certain period. You may choose to play the game for an hour or even an entire day—consider what's realistic for your kids' ages and personalities. Instead of talking, your children must use hand gestures to communicate, act out scenarios, or even mouth words to request assistance. Make this game a challenge by keeping score of who speaks or even giggles. The child who remains silent for the longest period wins that round. In order to keep the silence going, repeat the game until each child is declared a winner.

◯ CONSTRUCT BATHTUB SPEED BOATS

Make bath time much more fun for your younger children with bathtub speedboats. Find some empty milk or juice cartons and transform these household items into a toy to entertain your kids in the water. With adult supervision, have your kids cut the empty cartons in half vertically and slice a small hole in the bottom of the construction to serve as a drain. Blow up a balloon to serve as the sail for the boat, tie it at the end, and then secure it to the inside of the carton with duct tape or even glue. Lay the carton with the balloon in a bathtub full of water and watch as it zooms around. Let your kids get into the bath with the boats or lean over the tub to race a few of their newly constructed speed boats for a race they will remember.

○ CREATE STATIC ELECTRICITY

Have fun with balloons while teaching your children more about how electricity works with this activity. All you need is a few balloons to make this activity a teachable moment with a few laughs. Start by blowing up a few balloons. Once the balloons are ready, have your children rub a balloon on the side of their head. Next, ask the kids to hold the balloon away from their head while standing in front of a mirror to see their hair stand on end as it is attracted to the balloon surface. After this hair-raising moment, discuss how static electricity works, explaining that the static builds up on objects that are rubbed together and sometimes even creates a shock when you touch other objects. This activity is designed primarily for older children to avoid any potential risk of injury when playing with balloons.

○ IDENTIFY THE MISSING OBJECT

Help your kids improve their observational skills with this activity. With just a few household items or toys, you can launch a competitive game when the kids are bored. The goal of the game is to identify objects that are missing from a series. For example, line up a few household items on the kitchen table, such as a spatula, fork, napkin, and piece of bread. Then, have the first player turn around or close his eyes and ask one of the kids to remove an object. The player must then turn around and identify the object that is missing. Repeat the process with every player. You can also mix up the game by having your children retrieve objects from other rooms, such as small toys, stuffed animals, and board game pieces. A variation of this game is to place several objects on the table that are similar and one that doesn't fit into the theme. The player must identify which object is unlike the other.

○ MAKE A HOMEMADE CLAW MACHINE

AGES 6–12

You don't have to take the kids to the arcade to introduce them to the challenge of the Claw Machine. Instead, create your own claw challenge with tongs and a few household items or toys. Start by having your children gather small toys from their rooms or small items in your home, such as miniature stuffed animals, tennis balls, or even small toy cars. Place each item on the kitchen table and let your children take turns trying to pick up the objects with a pair of barbecue tongs. If you want to include an element of surprise to this activity, place all items in a large brown paper bag and have each player try to pick up items in the bag with the tongs. Use a bandana or towel to blindfold the players so they are surprised when their prize is revealed.

○ DESIGN A VELCRO GLOVE GAME

AGES 6–12

Velcro is a handy resource to have around the house, but when you can turn it into a fun outdoor or garage activity for the kids—even better. Simply grab a few pairs of cotton or flannel gloves set aside for the winter months, a Ping-Pong or tennis ball, and get ready for some fun with Velcro. The object of the game is to toss the balls to one another and catch them with just the Velcro strips. Prepare for the fun by putting a few strips of Velcro on the balls and on each pair of gloves. Then, it's time to toss the balls back and forth, catching the Velcro ball to the glove.

◯ MAKE PERSONALIZED MAGNETS

Make a craft that is worthy of being displayed on the fridge with this art project. From pictures of your friends, kids, or family members to illustrations and drawings of the family pet, you can make magnetic art for the fridge while making memories. First, grab a few fridge-worthy pics your kids want to display. Then, take an empty cereal box or piece of cardboard and glue the photos to it. Trim the pictures so they are covering the portion of the cardboard perfectly and then glue a few magnetic strips to the back of the cardboard. For a fancier look, consider covering the image and the cardboard with clear adhesive vinyl before attaching the magnetic strips. If you don't have any photos handy, your kids can also draw small illustrations on sheets of paper to attach to the cardboard and proudly display on the fridge.

◯ CREATE A HOMEMADE MOBILE

Mobiles aren't just for babies! Find a few clothes hangers and let your kids transform them into interesting mobiles that reflect their personalities. All you need are a few hangers, kid-friendly scissors, colored paper, glue, and some string to create a mobile. Begin by choosing a color for each child's hanger. Then, cut out strips of colored paper and add a few dots of glue to the hanger before wrapping the colored paper around the triangle part of the hanger. Next, ask the kids to find some trinkets they want to hang from the hangers, such as very small stuffed animals or paper-crafted ornaments. Using the yarn, tie the trinket to the bottom portion of the hanger. Hang these creations in your kids' rooms so they can admire their artwork.

○ PLAY HEADLINE ROULETTE

Inspire some laughs while prompting the kids to think creatively with a game of headline roulette. Simply pool together some newspapers or even magazines from your home, friends, or neighbors to get started. Using a few pairs of kid-friendly scissors, have the crew cut out large words in the newspapers or magazines. Each word should be cut into an individual piece and then placed into a bag or hat for later. Once the cutting frenzy is complete, divide the kids into groups and let each team member draw out a word or two. The team able to make the most interesting headline by piecing together the chosen words wins.

○ CREATE A TIME CAPSULE

While you can't keep your children small forever, you can preserve a piece of their youth with time capsules. Even though this activity takes less than an hour, the rewards will be evident years later when your family opens the time capsule. Have your kids think about items, notes, memorabilia, and photos that are important to them. If they are willing to part with a small toy, a personal photo, or even a school art project, put it in a sturdy shoe box or plastic bin. Ask relatives to bring by items to include in the time capsule as well, such as newspaper clippings or tokens from family vacations. Pick a spot to bury the box or bin in your backyard or place it in a corner of the attic. Don't forget to find it and open it in five or ten years.

○ COUNT LOLLIPOP LICKS

Even snacktime can be boring for children who love to be enter-tained. If your children are hungry for something sweet and looking for a game to play, consider breaking out some lollipops to keep them licking and laughing. You can stage this activity a couple of different ways—first as a challenge to see who can finish a lollipop first without biting into the core, and second as a way to help your children expand their counting abilities. Before handing out the lolli-pops, explain that they must count each lick aloud while working to finish the lollipop. Set the rules of the game to determine who wins. For example, you can award a prize for the player who counts the most licks or offer a reward to the child who finishes the lollipop first.

○ MAKE A SENSES JOURNAL

It's not always easy to be observant, especially when your kids are feeling antsy. However, a change of scenery and an activity that prompts them to record what they see, hear, smell, taste, and touch can help them get back in touch with their senses. Take a moment to sit outside on your patio or yard or venture to the park with a few notebooks in hand. Then, give each child a notebook and a pen or pencil. Instruct your children to take a minute or two and write down everything they see, hear, smell, etc. Little ones who have not yet mastered writing can also draw what their senses dictate. If you are outdoors, give them a few leaves or flowers to feel so they can jot down that sense too. The best thing about this activity is that you can help them observe senses in just about any environment.

○ MAKE UP A NEW HOLIDAY

AGES 6–12

Holidays are often exciting for children because it gives them a reason to celebrate, but if your children are bored and it isn't a holiday, create your own special holiday to keep them entertained. Start by brainstorming funny ideas for a holiday, such as ice cream day, blue day, or even dog day. Then, take the theme to the next level by outlining ways to celebrate. For example, if it is blue day, then everyone in the household must wear blue clothing and you can even add blue food coloring to your meals. If it's ice cream day, show the kids how to make homemade ice cream and host an ice cream party complete with toppings such as sprinkles, cookie crumbs, and strawberries. Give them a reason to celebrate and become the party planners for a day with this activity.

○ HOST A "JUST BECAUSE" SURPRISE PARTY

AGES 6–12

Most kids love to be surprised, but it can be even more fun for them to *plan* the surprise. With this activity, you get to show your children how good it feels to make someone else feel special "just because." Start by brainstorming people in your family or your neighborhood who you want to celebrate and reward. Maybe a grandparent has been especially helpful carting the kids around or a neighbor has been feeling low. Boost that special person's spirits by hosting a surprise party to honor her, complete with balloons, decorations, and even a cake or cupcakes. Have your kids start by choosing the honoree and then send them off to decorate a room in your home to launch the surprise. They can even help you bake brownies, cookies, or cupcakes for the party. Then, ask each child to make a homemade card to present to the honoree. The only thing left to do is invite the special person over and surprise her with a party in her honor.

○ PLAY THE CHORES GAME

It's often difficult to motivate your children when a day of cleaning is looming. Jump-start their willingness to clean their rooms, wipe down the kitchen counters, or even vacuum with this competitive activity. Use a timer to your advantage if your kids are motivated by competition. Gather all the children and write down a list of chores that require equal effort and time, writing down each chore on a strip of paper and then placing the strips into a hat or bowl. For instance, one task could be to vacuum the living room while another task could involve picking up the toys in the playroom. Next, have each child draw out a chore from the basket, bowl, or hat and set the timer for five minutes. Once the timer starts, send off each kid to complete the chore and the first one finished wins that round. Repeat the process until all chores have been completed for the day.

○ CREATE A FIX-IT BOX

When the kids are playing—inside or out—there are bound to be a few boo-boos from time to time. Get them involved in becoming the "fixers" with this activity that teaches them ways to be prepared. First, have the kids decorate a shoe box to create a makeshift first-aid box. Decorate the box with colored construction paper, label it the Fix-It box, and make a list of items to put inside the box. Next, stock up on what you need, such as bandages, first-aid ointment, adhesive tape, and wraps. Throw in some sunscreen or bug spray too.

○ MAKE AN IOU BOOK

Show your children the value of giving back by brainstorming ideas for an IOU book. Whether you choose to create these for family members or siblings, your kids can see just how small gestures can make a big difference. Gather a package of index cards or cut pieces of paper into small squares. Then, at the kitchen table, arm your children with markers and crayons to start crafting IOUs. While little ones who are still working on their spelling may prefer to draw pictures of what they plan to do, your older kids may want to write explanations of each gesture. Sample ideas include taking out the trash for Mom or Dad, pulling weeds for a neighbor, playing a game with a younger sibling, or doing an extra chore one day. You can keep these IOUs loose to distribute to multiple people or make an IOU book by compiling the cards or pieces of paper, punching holes in the side, and tying the book together with yarn.

○ PLAY SHOW ME HOW

Life skills are absolutely necessary for children of any age, but as a parent, you may not always know what types of things your children need to learn. Launch this activity to teach your kids what they want to know. To begin, have your children make a list of things they don't know how to do, such as loading the dishwasher, operating the washing machine, or even handling a small leaf blower. Once they have a list compiled, write each task on a piece of paper, cut the paper into strips, and put them in a hat. One by one, pull out a task and show your crew how to accomplish the task. Make this a hands-on activity by carefully supervising your children as they attempt to master these tasks.

2. ENJOY THE GREAT OUTDOORS

If electronics have kept your children inside soaking up the air conditioning instead of the sun, it's time to show them that playing outside can be just as exciting. With just a little bit of creativity and a few household items, you can show your children how to get wet and wild while staging a car wash or building a homemade Slip 'N Slide. Or, teach them how to concentrate while building an outdoor playing card tower or creating a customized driveway racetrack. Whether the sun is shining or the snow is falling, outdoor activities give your kids a chance to get a healthy dose of fresh air and exercise. From taking off into the woods to hunt for bugs (for some down-and-dirty quality time) to launching a litter patrol in a nearby park (to enhance the curb appeal of your community), these one hundred screen-free outdoor activities show your young kids how to let loose while under the sun—or the moon!

⭕ HAVE A JUMP ROPE CONTEST

Send the kids outside for a little fun with jump ropes. With just a little practice, even the smallest ones in your troop can master their skills and get a little exercise at the same time. See if anyone needs instructions for how to jump—it can be difficult for younger kids to get the hang of! Have each child practice individually to gain momentum and rhythm with each jump and then let a competition begin. Start by hosting a timed contest to see who can jump the longest when each child has his own individual jump rope or launch a group competition to see how many members of each team can jump in during double Dutch. You can even suggest a race where each player skips to the end of the driveway and back successfully.

⭕ BUILD AN OBSTACLE COURSE

Are the kids always using your living room furniture as an obstacle course? Move that fun outside! Guide your kids through the process of placing Hula-Hoops, boxes, slides, and cones in the garage or the driveway. Once the course is set up, host a race or a competition to see which kid can make it through the course in the least amount of time. Discuss the rules ahead of time so it is clear how many times you must Hula-Hoop, jump rope, hop over boxes, or navigate cones on foot or with a bike. If a rainy day puts a damper on your outdoor plans, then you can relent to creating a safe course inside by putting couch cushions on the floor and watch as your little ones hop over each one to reach the finish line.

○ STAGE A CAR WASH

While it may be difficult to get your children to mop the floors or vacuum on a regular basis, they probably won't mind washing your car! Have each child suit up in clothes that can get wet and gather buckets, soap, sponges, and old rags to stage a car wash in your driveway. Make cleaning fun when the sun is shining bright by breaking out the hose and helping your children fill up empty buckets with soap and water. Next, assign each child a portion of your vehicle to wash after fully spraying down the car. When the suds are dripping and begging for a rinse, take turns letting each kid spray down the car and each other to cool down. If your neighbors are nearby, they may just want to pull up their cars to get in on the cleaning action.

○ PLAY BACKYARD KICKBALL

When your kids have some energy to expel, a game of backyard kickball is a great option. You'll keep their feet moving and their competitive spirits in motion as well. Begin by creating bases in the backyard with easily available items, such as a piece of a cardboard box, a cone, a small pile of sticks, or a landmark in your yard like a tree stump. Station your kids and their friends at each base and assign a pitcher for the center of the field. Once teams are chosen, begin the game by having the pitcher roll the ball to the first kicker, who can send that ball flying. Just like a game of baseball, each player kicking strives to run the bases before being tagged out. Watch out for those fly balls because if the opposing team catches one in midair, the kicker is out.

○ MAKE AN OUTDOOR TWISTER BOARD

Even though Twister is usually an indoor game, you can make one
outside in a grassy area with some spray paint. Create your very own
Twister board by spraying small circles in the grass or on a tarp with
different colors of spray paint. You can also make six circles of green,
yellow, blue, and red in colored chalk on your driveway or sidewalk.
Once the board is ready to go, put strips of green, yellow, blue, and
red paper in a basket or hat and have each person draw out a color
to put either hands or feet on the designated circle. Before long, your
group will be twisted up in the middle of the yard or driveway while
laughter ensues.

○ RIDE THE TRAILS

If those bikes in the garage are collecting dust, it's time to free them
with a ride on the trails. Strap on those helmets and get pedaling.
Begin by locating a nearby bike trail that is safe for the ages of your
children. Outline a route for the entire family to follow and start pedaling while feeling the breeze blowing in your faces. If your community does not have a bike trail, map out a route along the sidewalk in
a safe area for the bike excursion. Practice bike safety and directional
signs while riding along the trails. For little ones struggling to master the art of riding, consider placing training wheels on their bike
wheels to simplify the journey. Pack a few snacks and plenty of water
in your bike baskets or a backpack to satisfy those cravings and thirsty
mouths.

○ HOST A SNOWBALL CONTEST

Just because the temperatures are cold and snow is falling, you don't have to limit screen-free activities to the indoor areas of your home. Bundle up the kids and get ready to test their arm strength with a snowball contest. Once the kids are appropriately bundled up, make a pile of snowballs. While a few of the kids are making snowballs, designate the older kids to create forts. You can create a full snow fort if the downfall is plentiful, or drag out cardboard boxes to create barriers if you only got a few inches. Divide the group into two teams and evenly distribute the snowballs. Once each child is safely secure behind the fort, start launching the snowballs in the air to see which team can dismantle the other team's fort first.

○ SEEK OUT THE STARS

Share the natural beauty the sky has to offer when the sun sets with an activity that requires creativity and silliness at the same time. Grab a few blankets and make beds in your yard or patio for a relaxing stargazing session. Teach your kids a thing or two about constellations by pointing out shapes in the sky. See if you or the kids can identify the well-known constellations, then challenge them a bit more by asking them to describe a shape they can see formed by the stars. From common shapes such as triangles and stars to one-eyed monsters, let your children dive into their creative minds to imagine more than just constellations. Once a shape is identified, get a little silly by making up stories about the animals, creatures, or monsters they see sprinkled through the night sky.

○ MAKE MUD PIES

AGES 6-10

Instead of messing up the kitchen making real food, let your children get messy outside while making mud pies. Prepare for this activity by having each child change into play clothes. Then, gather up small shovels or even beach toys for this baking extravaganza. With just a little bit of dirt and water, your kids can mix up mud pies within minutes. Make this a true hands-on activity by encouraging them to dig their hands directly into the soil to form the best pile of dirt. For a creative touch, add a little grass or a few rocks to the top of the pies to properly garnish the pie.

○ BECOME A SPORTS ANNOUNCER

AGES 8-12

If your kids are obsessed with sports, give them the chance to call the shots when hosting an outdoor obstacle course or friendly kickball game. Whether you are playing soccer in the backyard or basketball in your driveway, this activity is great for all ages. Start by delegating one child to serve as the announcer before the sports activity or obstacle course begins. Then, give the child a makeshift microphone, such as an empty paper towel roll, a hairbrush, or bottle of water. While the game is going, the "announcer" is responsible for calling the action play-by-play into the microphone for all to hear. Encourage her to make commentary and congratulate the players for their efforts. Once the game is over, choose a new announcer for the next round.

◯ HOST A WATER BALLOON TOSS

If there's one thing kids of all ages love, it's water balloons! Start by gathering up balloons left over from birthday parties or family gatherings. With the help of an adult, have each child wrap a balloon around the hose or a faucet to fill it halfway. Secure each balloon by tying the stem into a knot. Once you have a dozen or more balloons ready to go, have the kids choose a partner and line up the kids 10 feet from one another. And, the toss begins. See who can keep the toss going the longest without bursting the balloon or just sit back and admire the looks of surprise when the balloons burst in the air.

◯ BUILD A SLIP 'N SLIDE

When your kids are begging to go to the pool with the cool water slide but you have to stay home, show them just how fun it can be to create a water wonderland at home using household products. With just a few trash bags, tent stakes, and a hose, you can make a slide that offers tons of entertainment. Use duct tape to connect large trash bags in a line. Spread out the connected trash bags in the middle of the yard and secure them into the ground using tent stakes. You can use a flat area or an incline—just be sure your kids can handle whatever surface you're using. Drag out the hose and let the waterworks fully soak the trash bags. With a running start, children of all ages can get wet and wild within minutes. If the slide isn't slippery enough, add a few drops of dish soap to each trash bag to boost the sliding potential.

◯ HUNT FOR BUGS

Teach your little ones that bugs aren't icky with a bug hunt staged in your neighborhood or in your very own backyard. To start this activity, talk first about the types of bugs that exist in your area and show the kids pictures of common insects, such as ants or fireflies. Next, set out with digging tools to find the little critters. Follow the ants to an ant hill or play a game of chase following flying bugs in the park. This activity isn't limited to the daytime either. Lightning bugs roam at dusk or nighttime and are a little easier to spot or catch. Once your children have collected bugs, let siblings and friends admire the collection before freeing the bugs to roam back to their homes.

◯ GO ON A SOUND HUNT

If the only sounds you hear are sighs and groans of boredom and frustration, it's time to change the soundtrack of your day. Just like a scavenger hunt, make a list of common sounds you might hear outside and give each child a copy of the list. As a group, head out into the neighborhood or stroll around the park to find the sounds on the list. Common sounds may include birds or crickets chirping, dogs barking, lawn mowers chopping up grass, swings creaking, or doors slamming shut. If you live in a busy city, listen for sounds such as cars honking, motors revving, music playing, or church bells ringing. Add a competitive touch to this activity by awarding points for the first child to notify you when he or she hears a specific sound on the list.

○ CREATE SIDEWALK CHALK ART

When boredom sets in, give your child an almost limitless canvas for creativity with sidewalk chalk. If you need to allot space for multiple kids, create designated areas on your sidewalk or driveway so each child has a chance to draw a masterpiece. Stock up on sidewalk chalk in a variety of colors so your kids can draw flowers in bloom or sketch their bodies in white chalk. Feeling really ambitious? You can even make your own chalk the day before by mixing 1 cup Plaster of Paris, ¼ cup acrylic paint, and ¾ cup water. Pour the mixture into molds for the shape you desire (you can use small plastic cups or shaped molds) and let the mixture dry for twenty-four hours at room temperature. When your little artist's creativity runs dry, make a hopscotch court or draw games of tic-tac-toe to extend the fun.

○ PAINT ROCK PEOPLE

AGES 6-10

Add some personality to the rocks lying around in your landscaping or street with an art project that keeps your kids busy. First, gather up both small and large rocks to decorate and personalize. Once you have a pile of rocks, supply each child with acrylic paint, paintbrushes, or markers. Let your creative geniuses transform these rocks into people by drawing faces, hair, eyes, noses, and mouths. They can even customize clothing for the rocks and add striped patterns or even logos on the rock person's body. Have your kids put their names on the back of each rock creation and then set out to hide these rocks in special places for others to find. Many neighborhoods and communities host rock finds with clues for the search, ultimately leading your child to another child's creation.

○ CAMP IN THE BACKYARD

Love camping but don't like the hassle of driving everyone to a far-away location? Just find a patch of grass in your own yard, check the forecast for a dry night that's not too cold, and have a campout. Begin by gathering all the camping supplies you'll need for an eventful night in nature. If you have a tent, help the kids pitch it in a spot of their choice. If you don't have a tent, set up poles or large sticks and drape a sheet over the poles to make a canopy. Throw some sleeping bags in the "tent" and get the snacks ready for the camping excursion. If you can make a fire in your yard, let the older kids provide a meal for the little ones by putting potatoes in tin foil and cooking it over a campfire—then end the "meal" with s'mores, of course.

○ COLLECT AND MEASURE RAIN WATER

When rainfall has you and your kids feeling trapped inside for the day, weather the storm with an activity that offers a fun lesson in math too. If you don't have a rain gauge, you can make your own with just a few household items. Gather several empty 2-liter bottles and cut off the top portion of each bottle for your kids. Place a few pebbles into the bottles so they won't blow away. Take the top portions of the bottles and flip them over to fit in the bottom portion to act as a funnel. Then, pour just enough water into each bottle to cover the rocks. Place a piece of masking tape vertically on the bottle, starting where the water fill line is above the pebbles. Then, have the kids use a ruler to mark each centimeter. All that's left to do is place the bottles outside and wait for the rainfall. This activity can last for hours if the rain continues and can even offer a lesson in math when your kids tally the total amount of rainfall.

○ PLAY FLASHLIGHT TAG

AGES 8–12

If you need a way to entertain older children once the sun goes down, an old-fashioned game of flashlight tag may be just what they need to expel some energy. If you have handheld flashlights and an area free from tripping hazards, such as a backyard or small, safe park, you can set the kids off on an adventure under the stars. Flashlight tag is very similar to hide-and-seek, but the darkness and the flashlight add an interesting twist. To get started, designate one player as the person who seeks. The seeker gets the flashlight and counts to thirty while the other players hide in the designated area. When the seeker finds someone hiding, he or she must shine the flashlight on the player. Then, the roles reverse and that particular hider becomes the seeker and the process repeats.

○ WATER THE GRASS AND YOUR FRIENDS

AGES 6–12

Hot and sunny days can send even the most mild-mannered kids into fits of frustration. Water down the tension with an activity that offers nourishment to your yard and a sprinkle of smiles to your children's faces. All you need is a hose to water the grass and your kids with this activity. Have your children put on their swimming suits and flip-flops and venture out into the yard with a garden hose. Use this time to talk about how grass needs water to grow and allow each child a turn to water portions of your front and backyard. Once the grass is watered, turn the hose on the kids or let them take turns showering their friends with cool water. If you have a sprinkler, set it up and let them run through it to bring about fits of giggles.

○ DRY AND PRESS FLOWERS

Preserve the beauty of your blooming flower garden with an activity that leaves your children with a keepsake weeks later. Drying and pressing flowers may not provide immediate results, but the radiant colors preserved give your child something to cherish a bit later. Begin by having the kids each pick a few flowers from your flower garden. It is best to pick flowers on a sunny day so the petals are not wet. Bring the flowers inside and cut the stems at an angle. If the flowers are too large, tear off a few of the petals so they can easily lie flat. Line a large, heavy book (or a phone book, if you still have one!) with parchment paper and tape the flower to the paper. Close the book and put a weight or heavy object on top of the book so the flowers press firmly to the paper. In a few days, open up the book to find the pressed flowers. Peel the flowers from the parchment paper to place directly in a frame to preserve and display.

○ LAUNCH AN EGG TOSS

Although this activity may cause a few messes, the smiles and laughter make up for the time needed to clean up egg yolk. Have your children put on old clothes and pair off into teams. Each child should be standing directly across from his or her partner about 3 feet apart before beginning the egg toss. Break out a carton of eggs and give each team an egg to begin tossing. You can host a competition to see which team tosses the longest without cracking the egg or award prizes to the pairs who break the egg first. Add a bit of a challenge to the game by having each child take one large step backward after a successful throw to see how far they can get without breaking the egg when tossing.

○ RACE PAPER AIRPLANES

Send your kids' excitement level soaring with a paper airplane race. After a little time spent making and decorating the aircrafts, they can head outside to the races! Find a plain piece of construction paper for each child. Fold the paper in half lengthwise and immediately unfold it. Fold down both upper corners to the crease to form triangles. Continue to fold down the top triangle so the paper looks like an envelope. Again, fold down the top corners to form the nose of the plane and then fold the entire paper in half. Once the plane is complete, encourage your children to personalize their aircrafts with stickers, markers, or crayons. The only thing left to do is start flying the creations in the yard. Make this activity a friendly competition by hosting a race to see whose airplane flies the farthest in the yard.

○ MAKE A JUMPING PILE

Fall cleanup doesn't have to be met with moans and groans. Transform those leaves scattered around your yard into a pile of fun for the neighborhood kids. Make this activity a family affair from start to finish by supplying each child with a rake to gather leaves into a pile. Smaller children can even use plastic beach rakes or pick up leaves by the handful to add to the pile. Form a large circle with the leaves in a safe area of your yard and inspect the pile to make sure branches or rocks are not hidden in the center of the pile. Once the leaves are piled high, have each child run and jump into the pile before raking up the pile to get ready for the next jumper. You may find that family pets also want to take a dive into the pile after hearing the giggles.

○ PLAY LAWN-CHAIR MUSICAL CHAIRS

AGES 6–10

■□□

Showcase your children's speed and singing abilities with this fun-filled outdoor activity. You just need a few lawn chairs and a few singers to play this game of lawn-chair musical chairs. Begin by designating one child to choose a song to sing. Then, count how many remaining players you have, subtract one, and arrange that number of lawn chairs in a circle on the driveway or in the yard. Each child marches around the chairs while the leader is singing. Once the singer stops, each child must find a seat quickly. The child left standing is eliminated from the game. Repeat the process as the singer showcases his or her musical talents and pulls away yet another chair until only one chair is left. The last person sitting wins the game.

○ TIE-DYE A T-SHIRT

AGES 8–12

■■■

Brighten up a dreary day with a project that enhances your child's wardrobe. All you need is an old white T-shirt, acrylic paint, rubber bands, and a squirt bottle to unleash your kids' inner artists. Prepare your art station by mixing one part water with one part acrylic paint in a squirt bottle. You can also use a tie-dye paint kit. You can mix and match colors or make several bottles with various colors of paint for a colorful result. Dip the T-shirts in water and wring out excess water so each one is lightly damp. Set up a work station outside and help your children tie chunks of the shirt in rubber bands in various patterns on the T-shirts. Once the T-shirt is tied and ready to go, place it on a tarp and start squirting the paint onto the shirt using the squirt bottles. Allow the paint to dry for one hour before removing the rubber bands. The T-shirt should be almost dry at this point, but hanging it in the sun or putting it in the dryer for fifteen minutes will helps set the colors.

○ PLAY SIMON SAYS

When the kids are getting bored, see how well they can follow commands with a game of Simon Says. Choose one child to be the leader, otherwise known as Simon, and ask the remaining children to line up in a row to get ready to follow the instructions. Discuss the rules first and make sure they understand that if they do the action and the leader doesn't say "Simon Says" first, then they are eliminated from that round. Get creative by having the leader tell the other children to take steps forward or backward, hop along, run to tag a tree, or make silly faces. The object of the game is to be the last one remaining. Once the round is over, choose another leader to become Simon and let the fun start all over again.

○ BUILD A FORT

Building forts doesn't have to be reserved for indoor play on rainy days. Your children can build an outdoor fort that provides them with a place to play while roaming your yard. Start this activity by brainstorming items that would help construct an outdoor fort. From boxes or pieces of cardboard to old sheets and blankets draped over tent stakes to using a fence as a built-in wall, your children have lots of options. Once the materials are gathered, you may need some duct tape to secure cardboard boxes or blankets to line the floor of the fort. Personalize the fort by giving it a name and adding a sign with fort rules. When the fort is ready to go, the options for play are endless. Your children can host a secret meeting with their friends or read books in the comfort of their newfound hideout while enjoying the fresh air.

○ BALANCE TO THE FINISH LINE

AGES 8–12

■■□

Test out your kids' balancing skills with a game that results in a comical mess outdoors. This egg race requires concentration, but also produces loads of laughs. Begin by supplying each child with an egg balanced in the center of the spoon. Line up the children in a row and establish a finish line some distance away. Once the race begins, see who can make it to the finish line first without dropping the egg. To keep the fun going, you can also alter the rules to allow each child who drops an egg to race back to the starting line and get a new egg to catch up to the rest of the players.

○ PLAY HIDE-AND-SEEK WITH A TWIST

AGES 6–12

■■□

Hide-and-seek is clearly not a new game, but you can entertain your kids by taking this game to a new level. Mix in the classic game Telephone when playing an outdoor game of hide-and-seek to test your kids' memories and stealth-like skills. The object of the game is not only to find the hiders in your yard, but also to spread a message correctly from one player to the next. Start by having the "seeker" stand behind a tree with his or her eyes closed and think of a phrase to use for the game while the "hiders" find the perfect spots. Once the "seeker" finds the first player, he or she whispers the secret message to this player who is now the "seeker" until the next player is found. The original "seeker" heads back to home base to wait for the end of the game. Each "seeker" passes on the message to each player found until the game is over. The last "hider" must reveal the message. If the message is correct, then the last "hider" gets to choose the "seeker" for the next round, but if the message is jumbled, he or she becomes "it."

○ CRAFT CARDBOARD CARS

AGES 6-12

Make good use of large moving boxes by crafting cardboard cars with your kids. This activity requires the help of an adult, but it's well worth the effort! To get started, seal a large box on all but one side with packing tape. Using a box cutter or sharp scissors, cut a space for a car door on each side of the box, leaving the top flap free. Trim down the top flap to make a windshield for the vehicle that your little one can decorate. Next, attach paper plates to the bottom four sides of the cardboard box car with glue to serve as the wheels. You can even glue on plastic cups to the front of the box for the headlights. Once the structure is set, have your kids decorate their cardboard cars with paint, markers, or crayons. The only thing left to do is host a drive-in movie night in the garage or driveway.

○ JUGGLE FRUIT

AGES 8-12

Gather up a few pieces of round fruit such as oranges, apples, plums, peaches, and tangerines and get ready to host a circus of talent. Juggling is often a challenging task, so it's best to start little ones with just two pieces of fruit while standing in a grassy area. Have them practice tossing the two pieces of fruit in the air and catching them. Once they have mastered two, see if they can add a third piece of fruit into the mix to perfect their juggling act. Practice makes perfect with this activity and hosting a juggling contest outdoors eliminates the mess, especially when the fruit hits the ground and splatters juice. When your kids have successfully learned to juggle fruit, peel each piece and look for a smoothie recipe or two that will make good use of the bruised fruit!

○ PLAY THE SNOW-BLOWING GAME

You don't have to live near snow-covered mountains to blow snow. In fact, you can take advantage of sunny days and host a snow-blowing game outdoors with a few household supplies. With a bag of cotton balls and a few empty paper towel rolls, get the kids ready to cover the yard in snow. Simply set up a station in your yard or driveway and have them balance one or two cotton balls in one end of the empty paper towel roll. Have them blow through the tube and see how far the "snow" travels. Add a competitive edge to this activity by hosting a contest to see who can blow snow the farthest. Once the contest is over, have the kids pick up the cotton balls and start all over again.

○ HOST A HOPSCOTCH CONTEST

When your kids have too much energy, put it to use by engaging them in an activity that keeps them hopping. Using sidewalk chalk, draw a diagram with eight boxes, alternating between one box and two. Put a large number in each box, beginning with one and continuing until eight. To start the game, have your children line up to take turns hopping on one foot and then on both feet directly on the numbers of the court. For older children, pose more of a challenge by placing rocks on certain numbers that each child has to pick up in between hops.

○ MAKE A RING TOSS GAME

AGES 6-12

Toss out the electronics and make a homemade ring toss game for some outdoor fun. All you need is a few paper plates and empty paper towel rolls. Break out some kid-safe scissors and cut a large hole in the center of each paper plate to use as rings. Depending on how many children you have participating, you can make just three rings or twelve rings for the game; however, designate a certain number for each player. Save one paper plate to use as the base and glue an empty paper towel roll to it vertically. Place the base attached to the cardboard towel roll a few feet away from the children and let them take turns tossing the paper plate rings around the towel roll in your yard or on the sidewalk. Bring out their creative spirits by decorating the paper plate rings with stickers, markers, crayons, or acrylic paint before launching this outdoor activity.

○ CREATE A WATER BOTTLE BOWLING LANE

AGES 8-12

You don't have to take a trip to the local bowling alley to teach your children the basics of bowling. Instead, use water bottles and a ball to make your own alley in your garage or driveway. Determine whether or not to use empty water bottles or full water bottles before setting up each one into a triangle diagram at least 10 feet away from the starting line. (Try to situate the pins away from the street so balls don't roll into danger.) Older children may be able to knock down full bottles, while younger children may have more luck with empty bottles—and a stiff breeze may mean you want at least half-full bottles. Have each child roll a tennis ball, whiffle ball, or bouncy ball in a straight line to see how many "pins" or bottles fall to the ground.

○ HOST A BUBBLE GUM-BLOWING CONTEST

Many kids love bubble gum—take it outside for this activity. Offer your kids pieces of bubble gum and have them start chewing it. Next, practice blowing bubbles with the gum. For younger children, you may have to offer a few suggestions. For example, it is often easier to blow a bubble by closing your mouth and pushing the piece of gum flat against the teeth before slightly opening your mouth and blowing the gum around your tongue. Once each child gets the hang of blowing bubbles, host a contest to see who can blow the largest bubble. You can even provide prizes for silly tricks or funny faces while blowing.

○ PLAY OUTDOOR SCRABBLE

Test the minds of your children and their friends with an outdoor game that keeps them moving and thinking. With a large grassy area, garage, or driveway—and a wind-free day—your kids can create words and an afternoon of fun. Cut about seventy or so small squares of paper and have your kids put a letter of the alphabet on each one. It's best to have at least three papers for each letter of the alphabet. Assign points to each letter, just like in Scrabble. For example, vowels are worth one point, whereas letters such as *Z* or *X* are worth three points. Don't forget to add a few blank pages as a bonus. Once the papers are ready to go, head outside and have each child choose seven pieces. Designate a starting point for the game by drawing a star in the center of the outdoor game board with sidewalk chalk. Then, have the children take turns creating words with their letters and placing the papers on the board. Each player receives a new paper or letter for each page used until all letters have been used. At the end of the game, tally up points for each child to see who wins the game.

◯ TRACE YOUR BODY WITH CHALK

This creative outdoor art project leaves you with a personalized way to greet visitors to your home. Simply supply your children with sidewalk chalk and send them outside to trace their bodies. Partner up the kids and assign one person to trace and one person to lie down on the sidewalk or driveway. Have the tracer outline the first child's body, starting with the head and moving all the way down to the feet. Then, swap and draw the other child. Once the outline is connected, each child can then decorate the trace of his or her body with colorful designs. For example, they can draw hair, clothing, eyes, and mouths to see just how close they can mimic their features. Stir up some more giggles with this activity by having the children lie down in funny poses before their partners trace their body.

◯ PLAY DUCK, DUCK, GOOSE

Entertain your kids and their friends with an age-old game of Duck, Duck, Goose. This game of chase has been around for years, but the fun never gets old. Start by positioning the children in a circle while sitting on a grassy patch of your yard. Determine who gets to be the first player or leader. This child gets to walk around the perimeter of the circle of his siblings and friends gently tapping each person's head, saying "duck" or "goose." Once the leader says "goose," that child has to stand up and run around the circle in an attempt to gain his or her seat back if the leader doesn't land there first. Whomever is left standing gets to be the leader for the next round.

○ MAKE FLASHLIGHT SHADOW PUPPETS

AGES 6-12

When it's dark outside and your children need something to keep them entertained, whip out a few flashlights and let their creativity take over. From making rabbit ears on the wall of the garage to body shadows on the sidewalk, the options are plentiful. Once all of your children are out-side and ready to be entertained, designate one person to be the first owner of the flashlight and shine the light on the wall of the garage. Then the rest of the party can use their hands to let the shapes unfold. Your child can make a dog shadow by facing his palm to the wall while separating the pinky finger, folding in the index finger, and raising his thumb. Opt for a bunny shadow by making a fist and raising just two fingers. A butterfly shape is also a favorite. (Make this shape by putting both hands together at the thumbs and cupping all fingers inward.) See just how many shapes and animals your kids can come up with.

○ MAKE A SNOW MAZE

AGES 8-12

When snow is falling but it's not the right consistency for sledding, challenge your older kids to create a maze to exercise their bodies and their minds. Even with just a few inches of snow, you can help them create a path that leads to a prize. Start by mapping out the maze on a piece of paper with your children. Have them designate dead-ends and paths that lead to the finish line. Next, after bundling up for the cold temperatures, arm your children with snow shovels or plastic beach shovels to begin making the maze. The goal is to expose grass as the path. While your older kids are constructing the maze and working together to reach the end goal, have your little ones build a snowman right at the end of the maze. Once the grassy patch is ready, have each child crawl or walk their way through to see who can reach the snowman first.

○ HOST A HULA-HOOP CONTEST

Get those bodies moving with a Hula-Hoop contest for all ages. All you need is a grassy area of your yard and a few Hula-Hoops to put the moves into action. Begin by instructing each child how to Hula-Hoop. For some children it's difficult to find the exact rhythm of their hips to prevent that Hula-Hoop from falling to the ground. If you can, offer an example by doing it yourself. Break out the stopwatch and time each child to see who can Hula-Hoop the longest. You can also have the other participants count to add more intensity to the game. If the activity proves to be too difficult for younger children, consider arranging the Hula-Hoops into a pattern and having them hop through each hoop for some extra exercise.

○ BE THE GYMNAST

You don't have to have an Olympic medal to show off your flips, rolls, and somersaults. Show your children that they can be a gymnast, too, with some outdoor acrobatics in the front or backyard. Start off this outdoor activity by having each child warm up and stretch gently. Tight muscles can lead to injury, so it's best to keep them flexible from the beginning. Next, ask each child to show off his moves. Maybe one child can do a cartwheel perfectly while another can do a backbend. Empower your kids by designating each child to demonstrate an acrobatic move while teaching the others to mimic her actions. Add a bit of a challenge to this activity by asking the group to choreograph a routine so they can show off their skills to family and friends.

○ PLAY HORSE WITH YARD STICKS

Test your kids' imaginations with a farm game sure to evoke giggles from the start. All you need for this activity is a few yard sticks or small branches from the yard to transform your kids into horses. Spend some time educating your kids about horses. Have them mimic sounds horses make, name some popular varieties, and detail what horses eat. Next, break out a few yard sticks and show them how horses gallop. If you need more horse accessories, send them into the neighborhood to find large sticks they can place between their legs and use to gallop. Once the horses are ready to play, create an obstacle course with cones or rings in the yard or host a race by drawing start and finish lines in the driveway. Make sure each child keeps the yard stick in place and gallops just like a horse would.

○ HOST A NEWSPAPER SNOWBALL FIGHT

Are the kids bummed because it hasn't snowed yet? Even if the temperatures are warm, you can create a winter wonderland—with paper. Start by having each child crumple up sheets of newspaper to form a ball. Use tape or glue to keep the ball secure if the pages are not crisp enough. Once you have plenty of balls ready to go, divide the group into two teams. Have them build a fort out of cardboard boxes so they can hide their "snowballs" and their bodies once the snowball fight begins. Once the forts are ready, let the snowball fight begin. See just how many each child can throw to the other side. You can even create rules for the game where children are tagged out once they are hit with a "snowball."

○ MAKE PAPER PLATE SHIELDS

AGES 6–12
■□□

If you have some superheroes in your crew, help them create their very own shield for a day of play outdoors. With just a few paper plates, yarn, and art supplies, your kids can transform their daily play into a warrior's field while saving the neighborhood from villains. Begin by supplying each child with a white paper plate. Turn the plate over and have your child create her own crest—something that defines her chosen superhero. Add some color to the shield with markers and crayons or even acrylic paint and glitter glue. Then, punch a hole into each side of the paper plate and string through some yarn and tie it in the middle of the plate to create a makeshift handle for the shield. Then, send your superheroes out into the yard to defend their turf.

○ LAUNCH A BALLOON TENNIS GAME

AGES 8–12
■■□

Opt for a new way to play tennis without the court and the rackets. Instead, supply your children with balloons and fly swatters for a day of outdoor competition. Spend a few minutes preparing for the competitive matches by having each child blow up a few balloons. Then, draw a line on the driveway with sidewalk chalk to designate the net. Supply each child with a fly swatter and determine players for the tennis game. They can play one-on-one or as teams. Have the first player serve the ball by tapping the balloon with a fly swatter, and then let the opponent fire the balloon back over the net. The goal of the game is to keep the balloon off your side of the chalked line and keep it from touching the ground.

○ CREATE A DRIVEWAY RACETRACK

If you're finding Matchbox cars all over your home, take those little toys outside and create a racetrack to entertain your kids. You don't need expensive equipment or huge plastic toy sets to host a car race when you have small cars and sidewalk chalk. After gathering up enough cars for each child, have your kids choose an area of the driveway for their racetrack. Using sidewalk chalk, draw solid lines to mark the straight lanes, preferably on an incline to gain speed. After the racetrack is drawn, host races with the Matchbox cars. Little ones can bend over and physically move each car down the road while older children can use remote control cars to navigate the track. Host a race or let your kids make up their own challenges.

○ PLAY A BALLOON BOUNCE GAME

Use all of that hot air your children are storing by having each child blow up a few balloons. Once the balloons are ready to go, head outside and start the bounce challenge. Have each child attempt to bounce the balloons on the ground without popping them. Just like you would dribble a basketball, attempt to dribble the balloon to a designated spot or play a game of "keep away" while dribbling with just one balloon. You can even make start and finish lines with sidewalk chalk on a sidewalk or your driveway if your children are competitive. If the balloons pop, tap into the extras to start the game again.

○ WALK THE TIGHTROPE

If your children have aspirations of joining the circus, give them a chance to practice their balancing skills without the risk of injury. With a little creativity and some string or yarn, you can teach them how to walk a tightrope outside your home. First, find a straight portion of your driveway or the sidewalk. Have your kids string the yarn in a straight line for about 10 feet. Cut the yarn and create an additional strip with some curves wound in the path for an added challenge. Then, line up your children and let them try their hand at walking the tightrope putting one foot in front of the other. Designate one child to be the ringleader and have him add variations to the tightrope walk, such as clapping while balancing or hopping instead of walking.

○ HOST A BLOOMING FLOWER CONTEST

Though it takes some time for flowers to bloom, you can encourage your kids to take notice of their progress with this activity. Put those leftover ice pop sticks to good use while testing your kids' abilities to predict growth. Begin by washing used ice pop sticks or purchasing a package at your local craft store. Have your children write their names on one end of each stick. Then, head outside to identify flowers that are likely to bloom within the next few weeks. Have each child choose a plant that he thinks will bloom first and put his stick in the ground next to the flower. Each day, head out to the garden to monitor the growth. When the first flower blooms, the person who placed his or her stick next to it wins the challenge.

⭘ CONSTRUCT A FENCE COLLAGE

◼◼☐

Showcase your kids' artwork while letting them get creative outside if you have a stretch of fair weather ahead. With some art supplies, a large stretch of paper, and kids with artistic flair, you can bring a (temporary) colorful look to your fence. Simply tape a large sheet of white paper to a portion of your fence to serve as the canvas. Then, give the kids some watercolors, washable markers, crayons, or washable acrylic paint and paintbrushes to start creating a collaborative mural. You can even cut up colored pieces of construction paper into various sizes and have them glue the paper to the mural. For older kids, it may help to develop a theme first so they are all creating art that coordinates. When finished, step back and admire the final masterpiece.

⭘ CREATE CRAFTY SUNGLASSES

◼◼☐

Protect your kids' eyes and step up their style with this outdoor activity. Start by searching your home for some old plastic sunglasses or purchase a few at a nearby dollar store. Then, set up some art supplies on a table in the garage or driveway (e.g., felt, fabric, pipe cleaners, rhinestones, googly eyes, glue, and glitter) to give the kids options for personalizing their sunglasses. They can add a dab of glue to the rims of the lenses and sprinkle on some glitter, or bend pipe cleaners around the sides of the sunglasses for a fuzzy feel. Let each pair of sunglasses dry thoroughly before letting your children wear them around.

○ PLAY SPONGE TAG

When the weather is warm, have the kids put on their swimsuits and head outside for a game that cools them off using simple household supplies. Fill a few pails with water and clean sponges to launch this water-filled activity. Using string, yarn, or cones, designate a large circle in the middle of your yard as the playing area. Then, assign one child to be the leader and give her a sponge and a bucket of water. The leader's job is to dip the sponge into the water and toss the sponge within the circle while trying to "tag" one of the other players. If she misses, she must go grab the sponge, dunk it, and try again. If a child is tagged by the sponge, she then becomes the leader. Make sure that all the players know that they must stay within the designated area to remain active in the game.

○ HOST A JELL-O BASKETBALL GAME

Some kids love the colors, texture, and taste of Jell-O, but did you know you can also use this jiggly dessert for an outdoor game? Prepare the kids by having them put on play clothes or swimsuits because this activity can get messy. After making Jell-O in a rectangular dish, cut the gelatin into squares and take the Jell-O pieces outside. Line up a few pails in the driveway or front yard. Let each child take turns trying to toss the Jell-O squares into the pail while standing about 10 feet from the pail. Keep a tally of how many "baskets" each child makes to determine a winner once the toss is over. You can also vary this game by cutting the Jell-O into small cubes. Then, pair up the kids and have them try to toss the Jell-O into their partner's mouth. Once the Jell-O is gone, break out the hose to lightly spray down the kids and the driveway or yard.

○ FIND NATURE'S CRAYONS

Show your kids the beautiful colors nature has to offer with this art project. Supply your children with paper and black markers to get started and then lead them on a hunt to find "natural" crayons. Have each child decide on a theme. For example, with a black marker they can outline an animal, a garden, or even your home's exterior. Once they have their outlines ready on the white pieces of paper, start hunting through the yard for natural items they can use to color in their pictures. For instance, use a few pieces of grass to rub onto the paper for a green hue or use the petals from a purple flower for lighter colors. Dandelions are ideal for adding yellow to the art page while plump tomatoes growing in your garden can add light red hues. Let the masterpieces dry and then find a spot on your refrigerator to display their talent.

○ COOK SUN SNACKS

When the sun is beating down, take advantage of solar power and bake sweet treats! Begin by supplying each child with a large piece of black construction paper and a sheet of aluminum foil. Glue the foil to the construction paper and once it dries, have your kids roll up the paper with the foil on the inside to form a cylinder. With an adult's help, crack an egg into a small glass dish and put the dish inside the cylinder. Once the dish is inside the foil structure, wrap the entire cylinder with plastic wrap and set it directly in the sun to cook. Monitor the progress to see just how long it takes for the afternoon snack to bake. In 90°F temperatures, a large egg will cook in two hours, but lower temps may delay the process. For variations, you can also slice up some apples and sprinkle some cinnamon on them, or put some tortilla chips and some shredded cheese in the glass container.

○ TAKE A SPACE ADVENTURE

You don't have to sign up your kids for NASA camp to launch them into a space adventure when you can make the best of cold weather and create your own space station at home. Because bulky snow gear often resemble spacesuits, show your kids that they can become an astronaut in your own yard. Start by having kids put on bulky coats, snowsuits, boots, gloves, and even a bike helmet to serve as a space helmet. Then, using a wagon, create a spacecraft. Let each child take turns guiding the spacecraft through the yard or driveway. They can also search for "moon rocks" in your landscaping or pretend to discover another planet in the sky.

○ HOST A WINTER PICNIC

Picnics aren't just for warmer weather! In fact, some fresh air in the winter might be just what kids need to stay entertained and away from those tempting electronics. Plan your winter picnic by having the kids choose a special but simple meal to enjoy outside. Choose from basics such as sandwiches and juice boxes or bags of fruit or crudités. Then, bundle up the kids with winter coats, boots, jackets, gloves, and hats to protect them from the cold air and winds. Clear off a place on an outdoor table and start setting up your picnic. If you have a small barbecue or fire pit nearby, start a fire for your children and help them roast marshmallows to warm up a bit. Make sure an adult is nearby when the children are toasting their marshmallows.

○ HUNT FOR THE SMALLEST TREASURE

AGES 6–12

A magnifying glass can be an endless source of entertainment to kids of all ages. When you supply them with magnifying glasses for this activity, you can also teach them about the smallest bits of nature that often go unseen. Send the kids into grassy areas or flower beds in your yard or a nearby park to see what they can find and investigate up close with their magnifying glasses. From ants and flies to small blades of grass and worms in the dirt, the great outdoors gives your kids a landscape to investigate. Turn this activity into a competitive game by challenging your crew to find the smallest insect. You can pair up the kids or send them off on a solo adventure to see what they can find.

○ PUDDLE JUMP

AGES 6–10

Many kids love jumping *in* puddles. But what if you want the kids to stay dry while you're on your way somewhere? That's the time to enlist the puddle jumping game. Pretend the puddles are actually hot lava and encourage your kids to stay out of the water. See who can safely jump over a large puddle, or who can hopscotch over two puddles next to each other. Add a jump rope to the mix and see if they can hop over the puddles while jump roping—a task that may be best suited for your experienced jumpers. You can even launch a game of tag, challenging each child to avoid the puddles while chasing each other in the backyard.

○ PLAY SNOW PATH TAG

A winter wonderland doesn't have to stop your kids from getting active outdoors. In fact, this unique game of tag requires a snow-filled yard and a pair of snow boots. Once the kids are bundled up with coats, scarves, gloves, and boots, head outside to explain the rules of this game. Start by having your children stomp out a circle in the snow that is about 15 feet in diameter. Then, make four paths that cross through the center of the circle, similar to cutting pieces of a pie. To start the game, assign one child as the leader who is responsible for tagging the rest of the players. Have each kid start running through the paths to avoid the leader. The primary rule is that you cannot stray from the paths etched out in the snow. Once all players have been tagged and ejected from the game, assign a new leader and launch another round of snow path tag. Watch out for crashes!

○ TEST YOUR STACKING

If you have a bunch of plastic or disposable cups littering your home after snacktime, put them to good use with this stacking activity that you can make easy for younger kids or more challenging for older players. Wash each cup (or start with a package of new plastic cups) and let your kids test their stacking abilities. (Since wind can knock over the cups, consider hosting this stacking challenge on a breeze-free day, in the garage, or underneath a covered porch outside.) Younger kids can line theirs up in a row while older kids can build more elaborate towers. They can collaborate or make their own creations.

○ HOST AN OUTDOOR PILLOWCASE RACE

Re-create potato sack races at home—if you don't have burlap sacks, you can just use old pillowcases. Assign partners for the races and line up the children with the partners about 15 feet apart. This game works best when you line up the teams in a row. Have one player from each duo put their feet into the pillowcases, pulling them up so they can hold the edges by their sides. Once the kids are ready, start the race and let the kids jump to their partner and get out of the pillowcase. The partner must then get into the pillowcase and jump back to the other side. You can also host a pillowcase race without teams and create a finish line in the yard or your driveway.

○ CHOREOGRAPH A RAIN DANCE

AGES 6–12 ■□□

Teach your kids more about Native American heritage on those hot, sunny days with a rain dance that includes traditional steps the Pueblos, Navajo, Hopi, and Mojave tribes have used to encourage rainfall and help their crops grow. If you need a rain shower to cool down your area, see if your kids' moves can bring about some raindrops and some soul-searching, as this is commonly a spiritual activity. Before performing a rain dance, take a trip to the library to research the history behind the activity. A common rain dance involves two people positioned about 10 feet apart. Have your children pair off and line up in the yard or driveway. Then, have your children place their left foot forward while raising the right knee before stomping it on the ground. Have the children continue the movements, alternating feet, while moving toward each other. Some rain dances involve using the same moves while traveling in a circle.

○ HOST A SOCK TOSS

AGES 6-12
■☐☐

As you're matching up socks on laundry day, show your kids how to fold one sock inside the other to create a ball. Add a rubber band to the sock pair to secure it a bit better and then take the kids outside for a sock toss game. The object of this game is to toss the sock pair in the air to another child and then return the toss without the socks touching the ground, especially since you just got these fresh-smelling socks out of the dryer. You can play this game with just two children or open it up to more, tossing the socks to random players. If the sock hits the ground, then the player who tossed them is out of the game. When you are down to just one player, deem her the winner and start the toss all over again. Add a bit more of a challenge to this out-door game by bringing out laundry baskets and lining them up in the driveway. Assign points to each basket and have the kids try to toss the socks into the baskets to gain the most points for that round.

○ LAUNCH BALLOON RACES

AGES 8-12
■■■

Gather a few balloons, string, and straws and see just how much hot air your children have for this outdoor challenge. Line up the kids in a row and supply each one with a deflated balloon and plastic straws. Cut the plastic straws in half and tape the straw pieces into the entry point of the deflated balloons. Once the kids are ready to begin the game, challenge them to start blowing into the straw to inflate the balloon. The first one to completely inflate the balloon wins. Make this activity a bit more challenging and entertaining by playing Simon Says at the same time. For example, as they are trying to blow up the balloons, have another child shout out orders such as "Simon Says, jump."

○ PLAY SNOWY FOLLOW THE LEADER

Just because the temperatures are dropping and snow is falling, it doesn't mean your kids have to stay cooped up in your home. Instead, get out the snow boots, the ear muffs, gloves, and winter coats and head outside for an activity that will warm up your adventurous crew. Similar to follow the leader, this snowy game works best with two or more children. With fresh snow covering the ground in front of your home or at a nearby park serving as the blank canvas, your kids can follow the leader and mimic each other's actions. Start by designating one child as the leader for the first round of the game. Then, the leader starts trekking through the snow, making up his own actions along the way. For instance, he may make a snow angel or a snowball, or even do jumping jacks. The next child in line must mimic the leader's actions while following in his footsteps. If he or she falters, the next person in line gets a turn to be the leader. Once the final player reaches the leader, find a new fresh area of snow and appoint a new leader to launch this activity again.

○ PLAY ABC JUMP ROPE

Help your kids master their ABCs while also improving their hand-eye coordination with this outdoor activity. All you need to have is willing participants and a jump rope. The easiest version of this game is to have each child jump with the rope while naming each letter of the alphabet in order. The first player to finish the alphabet without missing a beat with the jump rope wins that round. For older children, you can add a complex component to the activity by picking a theme, such as animals, and having each child name an animal that starts with every letter of the alphabet in order while jumping. Let the kids choose a theme, too, so they are more familiar with the category.

○ PLAY SOAPY HOT POTATO

While hot potato is not necessarily a new game, you can put a new, clean twist on this activity with just a bar of soap and a group of kids ready for some outdoor fun. The object of the game is to toss the bar of soap quickly to one another, as if it is hot. Start by having all kids sit in a circle to prepare for the game. Designate one child as the host of the game—she is responsible for singing a tune while the players are tossing the soap to one another. Once the singing starts, have the kids quickly toss the soap in the air, rotating from left to right or across the circle. If one of the kids drops the soap, he has to sit out until the next round starts. Once the singer abruptly stops, the child who is holding the bar of soap then becomes the leader. Add a messy twist to this game by dipping the bar of soap into a bucket of water first, making it extra slippery before the game begins.

○ LAUNCH A GAME OF FRISBEE GOLF

If you have a few Frisbees lying around, get the kids active and moving outside with a game of Frisbee golf. Ideal for older children, this game tests your kids' abilities to throw, toss, and tally points. In a large open space in your yard or at the park, place an empty trash can in a centrally located place about 10 feet away from the players. Have each child line up with a Frisbee and one-by-one, let each one toss the Frisbee toward the basket, striving for a hole in one. If a hole in one is not achieved, all players must pick up their Frisbees and attempt again. Create the next station by moving the basket to a different location, allowing the kids to throw their Frisbees again. Tally points for each round, offering a point for each throw it takes to get the Frisbee into the basket. Then, at the end of the game, the player with the least amount of points wins.

⭕ STOMP GRAPES

Got some grapes that are no longer very fresh? Often an Italian tradition, this historical activity allows your kids to see just how much juice grapes produce. Prepare for this activity by having your kids put on play clothes, strip off their socks, and get their feet ready to stomp grapes. Have the kids separate the grapes from the vine and put them in a large plastic container. Then, give each child an opportunity to step into the container, stomping the grapes with his feet. While it may feel a bit odd to have the grapes filter in between their toes, the reactions from your children as they turn the fruit into juice is bound to be priceless. Make sure you lay down a towel in the garage or driveway next to the plastic container so your kids can dry their feet as they exit the grape stomp.

⭕ PLAY AIRPLANE

If your kids have wild imaginations and a love for flying, why not turn your yard into an airport runway? First, help your children create runway lanes in your backyard using yarn, string, or chalk. Then, ask your kids to gather a few sticks from the yard while you cut a few pieces of fabric into rectangular shapes. Use hot glue or string to attach the pieces of fabric to the ends of the sticks to create makeshift flags. Then, let your children's imaginations thrive as they wave the flags to signal incoming planes onto the runway. You can even designate one child to be the airplane and have him run down the runway while being guided by the flags.

○ LAUNCH A RED ROVER GAME

This age-old playground game has been around for ages for a reason—it's fun! In a large open area in the yard or at the neighborhood park, divide your kids into two even groups and have them line up horizontally facing each other about 30 feet apart. The first group of kids must determine who they want to call in the first round and then chant "Red Rover, Red Rover, send [Name] right over" while their arms are linked together. That child must then run toward the group and try to break one of the arm chains. If he does not break the chain, he joins the opposing team. If he does break the chain, he gets to take a player from the opposing team back to his group to join their chain. This game continues until two or fewer children are left on one team.

○ MAKE TWIG SCULPTURES

You can look at twigs in your yard as a nuisance, or you can see them as a medium for creating art! For this project, provide each child with a paper plate and some glue. Next, send them into the yard to find small twigs of different shapes and sizes. Once they return with an armful of twigs, encourage them to start arranging the twigs into a structure on the paper plates. While one child may glue together the twigs to form a building, another may line up the twigs to build a log cabin. Of course, it's okay to reshape the twigs by breaking or bending them as needed.

◯ CLIMB SMALL TREES

If you have children who are ready to flex their strength while climbing new heights, then a tree-climbing challenge is the perfect way to keep them entertained. Start by identifying a small tree in your yard or a nearby park and line up the kids to see who can climb to the first branch. To protect the kids' hands from scratches, have them wear gloves with grippers on the palm. Also, avoid having your children wear open-toed shoes like flip-flops to help protect their feet while climbing. Then, with an adult's assistance, help the kids try to navigate the small tree, climbing upward toward the first branch. Due to risk of injury, it's best to only let the kids climb as high as an adult can reach while carefully supervising the activity. You can also put a chair or stool near the tree to help hike the kids upward, especially with little ones.

◯ CRAFT LEAF STENCILS

Fall leaves, with their brilliant colors and interesting and varied shapes, are an endless source of art possibilities. Have each child find a few leaves of varying sizes while you set the stage for this art project in your garage, yard, or on the sidewalk. Then, lay down newspapers to protect the ground below. Cut a square of cardboard for each child to use, making sure the square is larger than the leaves your kids have chosen. Place a piece of white paper on the cardboard and put one leaf on top of the paper, taping the edges. Next, put a squirt of acrylic paint on a paper plate and pass out paintbrushes for the kids to decorate the page. Let them get creative, mixing colors while slopping the paint on the paper and the leaf. Once the paint dries, pull off the leaf to see an outline of a leaf surrounded by an array of colors.

○ PLAY CAPTURE THE FLAG

AGES 6-12

If the kids need some exercise and you have a woody area full of trees readily available perfect for hiding flags, get them ready to run for this exciting outdoor game. The object of the game is to hide your team's flag and then search for the other team's flag. Begin by grabbing a few scarves, handkerchiefs, or even an old, colorful T-shirt to serve as the flag for both teams. Then, divide the children equally into teams and send them off to hide their team's flags without letting the other players see their special hiding spot. If playing in a park, make sure you designate specific areas for play. Then, with players from both teams guarding their territory, the children can run and try to find the flag without getting caught or tagged by a team member from the opposing group. If caught, the player is taken to a designated spot, known as the "jail." However, if one of your team members tags you while you are in jail, you are freed. The game is over once the first flag is found.

○ CREATE A HUMAN FOOSBALL COURT

AGES 8-12

Do your kids like playing foosball at arcades? Show them how to make a life-size foosball game right in their own backyard. Help your kids tie yarn from one tree to another (or one fencepost to a tree—whatever works in your space) to create a place to stand and hold during the foosball game. You can also tie yarn to chairs lined up directly across from one another to make several rows of yarn to serve as the court. Then, line up the children playing on both teams so they are standing in a designated spot while holding on to the yarn. Toss a soccer ball into the court and let your children try to play a game of soccer, also known as foosball, while staying in their designated spots. The team able to kick the ball past the goalie gains a point.

○ JUGGLE A SOCCER BALL

The object of this activity is to see who can keep a soccer ball airborne for the longest. Start by having your children practice dribbling through the yard to get used to the touch of the soccer ball. Then, line up the children to try their skills at kicking the ball into the air multiple times using just their feet or their knees. Make sure you remind them that hands are off limit for this challenge. The child who can kick the ball into the air the most times wins that round.

○ PLAY A FOUR-SQUARES GAME

Transform your driveway into an athletic court with sidewalk chalk. Four squares is an interactive game that requires four players and a basketball. Make the court by drawing a large square and dividing it into four smaller squares. Then write the numbers 1 through 4 in each of the four smaller squares. For example, write 4 in the top left-hand corner, 1 on the top right, 3 on the bottom left, and 2 on the bottom right. Now your court is ready for play. Assign a square to each player and have them bounce the ball so it hits one of the squares and then is caught by another player for continuous play. If one of the players doesn't bounce the ball or fails to catch the ball, he is eliminated from the game. The last player standing wins the game.

○ HOST SPRAY BOTTLE BATTLES

AGES 6-12
■□□

You don't have to purchase expensive high-powered squirt guns for a little wet and wild fun in the sun. Instead, create your own using some old spray bottles and plain old water. Gather up a few unused spray bottles from your cleaning kit and rinse them out thoroughly. (Don't use any that contained toxins.) Next, fill up the bottles with water and make sure that the sprayers are in working order. Arm each child with a spray bottle full of water and determine the rules for the game. For instance, you can play a makeshift game of tag with one child squirting the spray bottle while trying to tag the other kids with water. Or, you can stipulate that they can all squirt each other but that they must not squirt toward eyes and ears. Or, try to squirt a specific spot on the driveway or sidewalk.

○ PLAY A GAME OF SHARKS AND MINNOWS

AGES 6-12
■■□

If tag is a popular game of choice when your kids are outside, they'll love this variation of tag, known as Sharks and Minnows. Begin by selecting one child as the leader, otherwise known as the shark. The remaining children playing will be the minnows. Designate a large area for play in your yard and then have the shark stand in the middle. The shark must say, "Fishy, fishy come out and play," and then all the minnows must slowly take steps toward the shark. When the shark yells "shark attack," all the minnows must try to get past the shark to reach the other side of the play area without getting tagged. If a minnow is tagged by the shark, then he assumes the role of a shark, making it doubly hard to get past the sharks. When only one minnow is left in the game, she becomes the primary shark for the next round of the game.

◯ PLAY MONKEY IN THE MIDDLE

AGES 6–12

This interactive game is perfect for large groups, especially when friends or family members are visiting. To start the game, assign one player to be the monkey who stands in the middle. Have the other children form a circle around the monkey. Then, the players in the circle must toss a ball or bean bag to one another, throwing it high enough so the monkey cannot catch it. The monkey can move all around the circle to try to capture the ball or bean bag, but cannot touch any of the other players. Once the monkey intercepts the ball, the player who threw it becomes the monkey in the middle for the next round.

◯ ORGANIZE BICYCLE RELAYS

AGES 8–12

When the kids want to go on a bike ride, add a competitive component to an otherwise solo activity to keep them entertained and moving. With just a bike and start and finish lines, let the races begin. Start by pairing up the cyclers into teams of two. Then, using sidewalk chalk, mark off the start and finish lines on a residential street that is being guarded by an adult to ensure safety for the riders. Place one rider of the duo at the finish line and one at the start line. Countdown to start the race and let the first rider cycle to the finish line. That rider must then high-five the partner waiting before the next rider can then proceed back to the starting line. Once all the riders know the route, launch a race with teams of cyclists and time the riders to determine the winner. Be sure the teams are evenly matched with kids of all ages mixed together.

○ PLAY KING OF THE FOREST

AGES 6–10
■■☐

Let your kids see what it feels like to be king for a day. To play this game, designate one child as the lion, who is the king of the forest. Then, let the other players choose to be another animal without telling the king. You may have a monkey in the group or a bird flitting around. Next, have the king of the forest stand in the center of the yard at a designed marker while the other children hide. To start the game, the king of the forest must roar loudly and the other children must make their chosen animal sound. The king can take only five steps from the designated spot to hear the sounds better and guess the animal of each child based on the sound. If he guesses correctly, the child making the sound must return to the home base. The last animal in the forest then becomes the king for the next round.

○ BEGIN A GAME OF FREEZE TAG

AGES 6–12
■■☐

If a plain-old game of tag has gotten old, then try this variation of tag where your children can mimic statues while trying not to giggle at their own poses. Freeze tag is also a valuable way to teach your children how to balance or stop in their tracks if they encounter a dangerous situation. To begin this outdoor activity, designate one child to be "it." The child who is "it" is responsible for tagging and freezing the other players. As your children are running around a chosen area in your yard or at a local playground, the person who is "it" must chase after them and tag them gently. Once a child is tagged, she must freeze in position, even if her arms are stretched outright or one leg is in the air. The other children still running rampant can unfreeze the players if they can get close enough without getting tagged by the "it" player. Once all players are frozen and the "it" person is deemed the winner, choose another player to lead and start the game all over again.

○ CREATE DRIVEWAY ART

Bring some curb appeal to your home with this outdoor activity designed for the budding artists in your family. Gather up a few paintbrushes and some sidewalk chalk for a day of colorful creations. Have your little artists start by creating large outlines of shapes with sidewalk chalk on a portion of your driveway or the sidewalk. For example, they can draw a long flower stem and large, open petals. Use different colored sidewalk chalk for the outlines. Then, wet the paintbrushes and have each child fill in the open areas of the petals by blending the colors of the sidewalk chalk. Brush from the outside of the outline to the center for best results. Stand back and admire the masterpiece before having the kids work on another collaborative driveway drawing.

○ PLAY RING-AROUND-THE-ROSY

Entertain your younger children with an age-old game of ring-around-the-rosy to turn your outdoor fun into a sing-along for all to enjoy. Start by having a group of children hold hands or link arms while forming a circle. While hopping, walking, or skipping along to the right, the group must chant the following song: "Ring around the rosy, a pocketful of posies. Ashes, ashes. We all fall down!" Once they say "down," everyone in the group must fall down to the ground. Once the kids have recovered from the fall, start the game all over again. You can even add a competitive element to this activity by eliminating the player who falls down last and continue playing until only one person is left.

○ MAKE AN ANT FARM

If your children aren't afraid of creepy crawlers, then this outdoor activity is a perfect idea. To make an ant farm, you'll need a large, clear plastic container, a small drinking glass that fits inside the container, and a piece of screen large enough to cover the top of the container. Once outside, have your kids fill up the container with dirt to create a base for the ants. Then, send them into the garden or a nearby area to gather a few ants. They may have to start digging in the ground to find the critters. Put the ants into the container and place a piece of screen over the container to provide the creatures with air. Next, monitor the ants each day and have your kids drop in small bits of fruits or vegetables as a snack. Over time, the ants will create a tunnel that will help your kids see their daily journeys firsthand. Be sure to only catch black ants; you don't want your children to accidentally get into a bed of fire ants!

○ PRACTICE TYING KNOTS

Not every child is equipped with the skills of a camper, Boy Scout, or Girl Scout. Prepare your children for outdoor adventures by teaching them how to tie several types of knots. Gather a few pieces of rope (or yarn, if you don't have rope) to practice these skills. Start with a simple knot. You can have them lay the rope or yarn on a flat surface on the sidewalk or garage floor, and then form a circle, pulling the left end over the right at the bottom. Next, have them push the left end of the rope under the circle on the right side and firmly pull the string or rope together. Give them a new type of challenge by introducing two pieces of rope to tie a square knot. Begin by having your children make a loop in the center of each of their pieces of rope. Then, face one loop to the left and one to the right. Put the right-hand loop over the left-hand loop and pull the ends of the rope from the bottom to the top loop and pull firmly to reveal a square knot.

○ CONSTRUCT A CLOTHESLINE

AGES 8-12
■■■

While the kids may not be keen on helping with laundry, show them how to make an outdoor clothesline to put their artwork on display. After creating a few coloring pages or drawings indoors, head outside to create a crafty, functional clothesline. Start by having the kids locate two trees in your yard that are a few feet apart. Next, help them use a tape measure to determine the distance between the trees. Take rope or a long line of string (yarn may be a bit too flimsy) and tie it to a strong branch of each tree. Next, decorate your clothesline by clipping the artwork to the string or rope using clothespins or even small binder clips.

○ MAKE SUN TEA

AGES 6-12
■□□

Although this activity is ideal for the early morning risers, the results will last with your crew all day long whenever their thirst needs to be quenched. Once the sun is shining, have your kids find a large glass pitcher and a few tea bags. You can also modify this activity and use individual mason jars for each child to enjoy a beverage of his own. Tear off the paper portion of the tea bags so only the bags and the strings attached are visible. Next, have your children fill up the glass pitcher or mason jars to the brim. Before attaching the lid, dangle one tea bag per mason jar or four to five bags per large glass container, and close the lid with the ends of the tea bag strings hanging outside the lid. Set the jars or pitcher directly in the sun on your porch or sidewalk, and within a few hours, when the jars get warm and brown, the tea is ready to serve.

○ BUILD A ROCK COLLECTION

If you have collectors in your crew, keep them busy outside compiling a collection that teaches them more about rocks. Using household items and empty egg cartons, you can help your kids create a collection worthy of presenting at show and tell. If you have a library book that identifies types of rocks and minerals, you can expand this activity into an educational experience. The first priority is launching a search through your yard, local park, or neighborhood to find different types of rocks. Give each child a bag to collect her treasures and then head back home to help your kids polish them with clear nail polish to make each one shiny. Using an egg carton for each child, sort the rocks and put one in each egg slot. Using a small piece of paper, write down each type of rock after researching it in your library book. Then, with glue, attach each piece of paper to the inside of the egg carton, directly coordinating with the type of rock so each one is clearly labeled.

○ PLAY FROG AND FLIES

When ordinary games of tag aren't doing the trick, introduce your kids to a game of Frogs and Flies. This game encourages leaping and flying. Gather your group and head outside to a large, open area. Designate one spot of your yard to be the base, such as a tree or the front porch. Next, have the kids form a circle and assign one child to serve as the frog, who crouches down in the center of the circle. Once the frog starts leaping, the object is for him to tag the other children, the flies, as they roam around the yard. The flies can momentarily hold on to the base, the safe place, when tired. The last fly tagged serves as the frog for the next round of the game.

○ CREATE A CAN TOSS

Those empty tin cans in your recycling bin can come in handy for this activity when the kids need some outdoor entertainment. Simply remove the labels from three to five cans and have the kids number each one in order (1, 2, 3, etc.) with a permanent marker to get ready for this game. Next, line up each can in your driveway, on the sidewalk, or in the grass so the cans are at least 10 feet apart. Arm the kids with small nuts, stones, rubber balls, or tiny acorns to throw. Then, line up each child about 10 feet from each can in a single row. Each child gets a chance to toss an object into each can before moving to the next can. Have a scorekeeper keep track of the objects that made it into the cans and add the corresponding number of points listed on the cans to each child's overall score. The kid with the most points wins that round.

○ CRAFT A WALKING STICK

Nature offers us many useful resources. Show your children how to create a walking stick for those long hikes you love to take by using what nature has to offer. The first priority is to find a stick or straight branch for each child. Walk through the woods near your home or at a community park to find just the right size stick. Next, have an adult use a small knife to shave off any protruding areas that could scratch the kids. Before taking off with this walking aid, have your children personalize their sticks. You can use string to attach small bells, stuffed animals, or toys. Or, you could glue fabric or wrap yarn around the top of the sticks to offer a softer resting area for your kids' hands. The only thing left to do is venture out on a hike with their newfound walking sticks.

○ BUILD A BERRY BUCKET

AGES 6-12

Make an outdoor hike through the woods much more interesting when searching for berries. Before heading out to the wilderness, gather empty milk or juice jugs to prepare the buckets. You or another adult should cut away a small part of the jug, leaving the handle intact and the bottom portion of the bucket secure. Your children can decorate their buckets with markers or even glue drawings on construction paper to the bucket. Then, with the buckets in hand, head out on your morning walk or trek on a local hiking trail. While searching for berries to fill up the buckets, have each child consult with an adult who is knowledgeable about the types of berries that are safe to eat. Then, once the buckets are full, head home to thoroughly clean these sweet treats for your afternoon snack.

○ HOST AN OUTDOOR DANCE PARTY

AGES 6-12

Prompt your children to show off their dance moves with an outdoor dance party designed for their friends and siblings. With an even number of children, pair off the crew into groups of two and have them begin choreographing a routine to one of their favorite songs. You don't need electronics to keep the beats going when your kids can express themselves vocally and physically. Designate one pair of children as the beat boxers or singers and then another pair of kids as the dancing duo. Have all four work together to coordinate a dance routine and then put on a show in the driveway. Show them a few of your favorite dance moves, too, so they can incorporate something unique into the routine. You can also have the kids put together multiple numbers to showcase for Mom and Dad later, as well as a final number that includes everyone attending the outdoor dance party.

3. SUPPORT YOUR COMMUNITY

Teach your children the value of lending a helping hand in your community with these one hundred screen-free activities that allow them to volunteer their time and share their talents. From hosting a food drive to crafting a map of the city for new neighbors, these activities show your children how just a few hours can make a difference in the lives of those around them. Get your mini-me gardener excited about building a community garden, motivate your eco-friendly kids to find recyclable items, or help your child develop a nurturing personality while hosting a storytime session for neighborhood children. This chapter focuses on ways to keep your kids busy—with a purpose. With an activity that is designed to bring your children *and* others smiles, you can't go wrong.

○ VOLUNTEER AT AN ANIMAL SHELTER

AGES 6–12

■ ■ □

Teach your children—young and not-so-young—the benefits of helping cute and cuddly critters by taking a family trip to an animal shelter. Not only can you spend time with your children petting dogs and cradling cats, but you can also teach them how to care for others. Contact your local animal shelter or Humane Society to determine their needs before setting out on this adventure. If it's okay with them, take along treats or pet supplies to donate and have your kids present the staff at the animal shelter with the items you bring. Spend the afternoon taking turns walking dogs, playing with the kitties, or snuggling up next to a few frightened critters. Your little animal lovers will get the benefit of being a pet parent for the day, and the pets get an afternoon of love!

○ CREATE ACTIVITY BAGS FOR NURSING HOMES

AGES 8–12

■ □ □

Young children don't always understand why older people can't do the same activities that they can. Begin by talking about how older people usually lose some of their hand-eye coordination and hearing. Then, identify activities that they would still enjoy. Your kids can create blank homemade tic-tac-toe boards on construction paper or cut out large-print crosswords from magazines or newspapers. You might also consider buying an adult coloring book and having your children supply crayons and markers from their collection. If you're stumped, call a local nursing home and ask them for suggestions. Once the bags are packed, call ahead to let the home know of your plans, then deliver these goodies with your children to see the surprise and happiness on the faces of local nursing home residents. They might even want your kids to sit down and join them in the fun!

○ COMPILE CARE PACKAGES FOR SOLDIERS

AGES 8–12
■□□

Show your support for the armed forces by making care packages with your children for soldiers deployed overseas. Get in touch with local nonprofit organizations or contact a local military base to find out what type of supplies are needed and how the packages should be prepared. Then, send your kids on a scavenger hunt to find items to include in the care packages. Soldiers are often in need of hygiene items such as toothpaste, baby powder, deodorant, and shaving cream, and clothes like cotton socks. If you don't have these unopened items on hand, you can always take a trip to the local store to let your kids pick out toiletries. Add a personal touch to your package by having each kid write a letter of gratitude or color a picture.

○ BAKE COOKIES FOR FIRE STATION EMPLOYEES

AGES 8–12
■■■

Teach your kids to thank first responders by offering a tasty treat to the local firefighters and fire station employees. Whip up a homemade batch of cookies together or simplify the task for younger children by buying prepackaged cookie dough to bake. With some adult supervision, your children can get creative when making sweet treats. Choose from a roll of chocolate chip cookie dough or use cookie cutters to add unique shapes to a roll of sugar cookie dough. While the baked goods are cooking and cooling on a rack, have your children design ziplock bags to store them in. They can add a creative design or write a short note of appreciation in marker. When cooled, separate the cookies into bags so each employee can easily grab one. Next, arrange a time to drop off the goodies and take the kiddos with you to see the smiles their baked goods bring to the men and women who fight fires. If you time it right, your children may just get a tour of the firehouse.

○ BUILD A COMMUNITY FLOWER GARDEN

If your kids have green thumbs, let them share their time and talents with the community. With just a few gardening supplies and permission from your neighborhood or local city council, you and your children can beautify the city with minimal effort. Gather tools such as small shovels, gardening gloves, and flower seeds, and ask for permission to plant on the property. Then start weeding out those unwanted sprouts of grass and use a handheld shovel to dig the perfect holes to plant flower seeds. Space the seeds at least an inch apart, or purchase partially grown flowers to create instant beauty. Once the seeds or flowers are planted, make a schedule for each week for your little gardeners to water and weed this community flower garden.

○ SHOP FOR SHELTERS

Teach your kids the value of food while showing them how good it feels to give to the less fortunate. It is likely your local shelters are in need of nonperishable food, so with this activity, your kids can help meet the demand. Start by discussing what types of food are best to donate, such as canned vegetables, boxed mixes, and granola or protein bars. Make a list of the foods you want to purchase or request from family members before heading out to the store. Have each child sort through the weekly sales ads from the grocery store once you arrive to determine the best buys. You can supply each kid with a certain amount of money and challenge older kids to find as many nonperishable food items they can with the provided cash. Once the groceries are purchased, collect donations from family members before dropping them off at your local shelters.

○ COLLECT COATS TO DONATE

When the temperatures are frigid, it's an ideal time to talk to your kids about their desires to help those in need. Homeless shelters are often in need of warm winter coats, gloves, and scarves. Have your kids start by digging through their own closets for gently used cold weather items. Next, make some flyers to hang up in your neighborhood or community advertising that you are collecting coats. Once you have a hefty collection of winter coats and warm-weather clothing, contact local organizations such as the American Red Cross or Goodwill to determine how to deliver the goods. Take your kids along to show them just how much their efforts are appreciated.

○ CREATE A DIY TIC-TAC-TOE BOARD

Supply older neighbors with a game that your children can play with them again and again. With just some glue, fabric or wrapping paper, and a little time, your kids can whip up a tic-tac-toe game board and deliver the fun right to your neighbors' doors. Start by having your kids cut a piece of thick construction paper or cardboard into a large square to serve as the game board. Let their creativity thrive when choosing how to decorate the tic-tac-toe board. They can glue colorful squares of fabric to make nine different squares on the board or wrap the entire board in wrapping paper using glue or tape. Once the board is decorated, have your child draw lines on the board to separate nine even squares on the surface. Then, glue on wood sticks over the lines to make a separation. Let the board dry and decide on two distinct types of playing pieces. They could be almost anything, from small rocks to board game pieces. The only thing left to do is knock on a neighbor's door and launch a few intense matches of tic-tac-toe.

○ WEED FOR YOUR NEIGHBORS

You don't have to be an expert gardener to spend some time offering your services to neighbors in need. All your children require is a few gardening gloves, handheld shovels, and a yard waste bag to beautify the yards of those who are unable to maintain their home's curb appeal for one reason or another. Have an adult contact elderly neighbors and ask if they would like assistance with maintaining their lawns and flower beds. Once you have approval, discuss the best way to remove weeds with your children. Arm each one with a pair of gardening gloves to protect their hands from allergies, dust, or poison ivy and set off to the neighbor's home. Have each child choose a section of the yard to work on so everyone has their own space. Collect all the weeds in a paper lawn bag to dispose of properly.

○ FIND RECYCLABLE HOUSEHOLD ITEMS

Teach your children how to preserve the environment by launching a scavenger hunt in your home to find recyclable household items. After a briefing discussing what type of items are recyclable, send off each child with a bag to find the goodies. First, look for empty water bottles and soda cans hanging around in bedrooms or the living spaces of your home. Then, move into the pantry to condense large cereal boxes. Put all cereal or snack items into large freezer bags or Tupperware containers so the boxes can be recycled. Once your troop has a collection gathered, head into the driveway or garage to begin breaking down the boxes and crushing soda cans and water bottles to save more space in your recycling bin. You can transport these items to a recycling center or set them out for pickup if your city picks up directly from your curb.

○ HOST A BICYCLE PARADE

Offer goodwill and an entertaining show for your neighbors or community by having your children host a bicycle parade. To prepare for this exciting event, have your children and those around the neighborhood determine a theme for their parade. If it is during the summer, consider celebrating the Fourth of July and decorating the bicycles with red, white, and blue streamers and pipe cleaners. Or, you can choose an animal theme and have the kids decorate their bikes with animal accents, like ears fastened to the handlebars. Add in a few costumes to the mix and you have a full-blown animal parade. Make sure you have a large audience by making flyers announcing the parade ahead of time. Before setting out to entertain the masses, gather some party favors or candy your children can share with bystanders along the bicycle parade path. All that is left to do is pedal down the road, toss out treats, and wave to the neighbors.

○ SHOW YOUR TEAM SPIRIT

Your kids know how good it feels to see family and friends in the stands when participating in athletic events. Help your children make others feel good by showing their team spirit while also supporting the community. Brainstorm local sporting events that are probably not as well attended, such as high school swimming, volleyball, or softball games. Choose a team to root for and then deck out the kids in the team's colors. Make posters or flags to use when cheering on the players. During the game, encourage the kids to shout words of praise while clapping loudly so the players feel as if they are playing in a professional game with thousands of fans.

○ MAKE BINGO BOARDS FOR NURSING HOMES ■ ■ □

Bingo is often a popular activity at assisted living centers and nursing homes. Bring a colorful and creative touch to this popular game by having your children make personalized bingo boards for residents. Supply each child with square pieces of construction paper. To make a more sturdy card, you can use cardstock paper or laminate the construction paper. Have each child draw a five-column grid and label one letter (B, I, N, G, O) on the top of each column. Next, the kids need to draw five additional rows under the BINGO header to insert random numbers. While older kids can easily follow the numbers, you may have to provide a list for your younger bingo players. For example, numbers 1–15 are reserved for B, numbers 16–30 for I, numbers 31–45 for N, numbers 46–60 for G, and numbers 61–75 for O. Each child can randomly add numbers with a marker or crayon. Don't forget to add the free space on each card before delivering these handy cards to your local nursing home.

○ WALK NEIGHBORHOOD DOGS ■ ■ □

The young dog lovers in your family will gladly put down the electronics to take part in this activity. Begin by contacting a few neighbors to see if they need assistance with walking their dogs. Older neighbors, especially, may find it difficult to provide their pets with the exercise they need. Once you have identified a few available pets, arrange to have your children pop over at an agreed upon time to take little Fido on his walk. Supply the kids with plastic bags to clean up after the animals and discuss the importance of safety when walking near the street. If you have a few requests for the day, consider scheduling the walks separately just in case neighborhood dogs are not willing to play well together.

○ TAKE A TOUR OF THE POLICE DEPARTMENT

AGES 6–12

■□□

Give your kids a close-up look at the ins and outs of law enforcement by scheduling a tour of the local police department. Contact the department on the nonemergency line and inquire about scheduled tours or available times your family can visit. Expand the group to include your kids' friends or family members. To prepare for the trip, have a discussion with your children about the duties of police officers and dispatchers and ask them to compile questions to ask once the tour is over. You can also have each child draw a picture or write a thank-you note to deliver to the officers on the big day.

○ STUFF HOLIDAY STOCKINGS

AGES 6–12

■■□

Not everyone wakes up on Christmas morning with a stocking full of goodies. But, you and your children can increase their odds when stuffing holiday stockings and donating them to local outreach agencies. Begin by sorting through your holiday decorations to find extra stockings you can use for this activity. Use fabric markers to decorate the outside of stockings that are solid colored or plain. You can even help the little ones cut felt shapes to glue on the outside of the stockings. Next, prompt your kids to think about items that would bring cheer to others during the holiday season. For instance, include small pieces of nut-free candy, new art supplies such as crayons or markers, toy cars or figurines, and kind notes that spread holiday cheer. If you have an extra coloring or activity book lying around your home, toss that in the stocking too. Your children can also search their rooms for small toys that are new or gently used to stuff into the stockings. Once the stockings are full, contact a local resource agency that distributes stockings to children in need to donate your items.

MAKE CARDS FOR OUT-OF-TOWN RELATIVES

■□□

Grandmas, grandpas, aunts, and uncles love to hear from out-of-town family. With this activity your children can spread goodwill and keep your relatives up to date on their everyday activities while also bringing a smile to their faces when they receive letters from afar. You don't need to have fancy stationery for this activity. Instead, let your kids get creative by making cards from construction paper or cardstock you have lying around your home. Supply them with pens, pencils, markers, and crayons so they can make illustrations on each piece of paper. You and the kids can brainstorm what to say or information to share before adding text to each card. Help the younger ones with spelling or let them express their own thoughts in their own way before putting a postage stamp on the envelope and forwarding the cards to out-of-town family members.

DONATE LIGHTLY USED TOYS TO CHARITY ■□□

Your children probably have bins overflowing with toys that haven't been touched for months. Launch the cleanup crew to minimize the clutter and make a donation to charity that can positively impact the lives of other children. Teach the importance of giving back to others by discussing just how lucky your children are to have rooms filled with toys. Explain that some children in destitute communities aren't as fortunate. Once your children recognize that they have been provided with more than they need, it's time to arm them with bags to gather gently used toys that they no longer want or need. Inspect each toy to make sure it is clean or take some time to wipe down plastic toys with disinfectant cloths. When the bags are ready for delivery, contact local outreach agencies to determine the best day and time to deliver the toys.

○ HOST A LEMONADE STAND

Sweeten a sunny day with a fun activity that teaches your children about giving back to the less fortunate in the community while providing refreshments for people passing by. A lemonade stand is easy to construct and your profits can benefit local organizations. All you need is a few lemons to make freshly squeezed lemonade, or a prepackaged mix and a pitcher. Spend some time thinking about the setup of the stand first—you might have a small folding table that will work well. Have your children determine a good cause in your community that could benefit from a cash donation and then make signs advertising that all profits will be donated to this cause. Set up a small table on the curb or in your front yard and grab some plastic cups. Fill up a cooler or bowl of ice and set the pitcher of lemonade in full view. If the temperatures are heating up, prop up a few umbrellas to offer your kids some shade while they pour lemonade and seek out donations for a worthy cause.

○ WRITE KIND MESSAGES IN SIDEWALK CHALK

Sometimes people need to be reminded of the positive things in life. Your children could probably use a reminder, too, when they are whining about having "nothing to do." This activity gives them the opportunity to spread goodwill and get creative at the same time. With a bucket of sidewalk chalk and a few inspirational quotes or phrases, you can send them off to a nearby sidewalk or community area to cheer up area residents. Begin by brainstorming some nice phrases that make people feel good such as "You are beautiful" or "Make today a great day." Then, have them start writing these messages on public concrete areas of your community for all to see. Make sure that they do not decorate private property or driveways without permission.

○ CREATE A NEIGHBOR WELCOME BAG

Welcome neighbors into your community and keep your kids occupied for a few hours with this activity that is designed to show them how good it feels to make others feel valued. Have your little ones decorate paper bags with wrapping paper or colored construction paper before they start filling it with welcoming contents. Scour through your pantry to find tasty treats such as candy, packaged muffins or cookies, or boxes of brownie mix to include. Even better, if you can, find something local—homemade jam from a market up the street or local honey from a nearby farm. The best part of this activity is the joy your kids experience when delivering these goodie bags to the new neighbors.

○ PACK SURVIVAL BAGS FOR A WOMEN'S SHELTER

You may or may not be ready to discuss women's shelters with your kids. If you are, you can talk in age-appropriate terms about what you're going to do. If you're not ready, you can still collect these items and tell children they're for people who need them in an emergency. Discuss with your children what type of supplies are needed for daily survival. For example, you can include hygiene items such as toothbrushes, toothpaste, deodorant, soap, and brushes or combs. Basic clothing items such as new underwear or socks are often needed too. While you may not have all of these items on hand, it is possible to pool together a few dollars and visit a nearby store to pick up the remaining accessories. Once you have the items ready to go, decorate bags before packing up the supplies to add a bit of color and cheer to the package. If you feel comfortable having them do so, your kids can even write personal notes with phrases such as "Thinking about you" and "You are not alone" to give these women a moment of peace.

○ VOLUNTEER AT A FOOD PANTRY

Put your budding chefs to work with some volunteer work at a local food pantry. A few hours of help can make a significant difference in the lives of others. First, contact food pantries in your area to see if they allow kids to help. If they do, go through your own pantry to find nonperishable food that you can donate. Bag the donations and head out for a day to offer your services to the hungry and less fortunate. Younger children can help stack canned goods and boxed food on shelves at the food pantry while older children can bag items for food pantry recipients. If the pantry also serves food, your children might be able to volunteer serving food, emptying trash, setting up placemats, or making drinks. The experience is one they will remember and one that makes a difference in your community.

○ DECORATE MEALS ON WHEELS BAGS

Add a little color to the lives of those receiving meals from outreach agencies with this activity. Contact your local Meals on Wheels representative to determine the types of bags the organization uses to deliver food. In most cases you can use large brown paper bags. If you have a few on hand, you can get started right away or if needed, contact a local grocery store to get the bags you need. Then, encourage your kids to begin decorating. Wrap the bags in colored construction paper or cheerful wrapping paper. Have little ones glue on buttons or add a touch of glitter to the design. Offer an inspirational message for the recipients on the bag, such as "Enjoy your meal" or "Made with love." Once the decorated bags are ready to go, drop them off at the nearest Meals on Wheels office.

○ COLLECT SUITCASES FOR FOSTER CHILDREN

AGES 8–12

Many children who are removed from their homes or put in foster care have their belongings in a trash bag. Have your children help provide them with a sense of having something of their own by collecting gently used duffel bags and suitcases from people in your community. Market their efforts by having your kids make posters to hang around town or by having an adult post information about the collection on a local social media forum. Include an adult's contact number and note any organizations you plan to provide the suitcases to, such as social service agencies. You might even want to bring your kids to neighborhood yard sales to ask if the sellers will donate suitcases or bags from their sale. Once you have a hearty collection of bags, personalize each one with notes of encouragement tucked away in the pockets or compartments. Letters from your children can provide a scared child with a moment of peace.

○ CRAFT VALENTINES

AGES 8–12

It doesn't have to be the middle of February for your kids to show love to friends, family members, and neighbors. Start by gathering art supplies to craft homemade Valentines. Load up your kitchen table with construction paper, stickers, glue, paper doilies, markers, crayons, kid-friendly scissors, and even glitter so your children can get creative while expressing their gratitude to others without even having to say "Happy Valentine's Day." Brainstorm sweet messages they can send to grandparents, older neighbors, or even people who serve in your community. Deliver the Valentines to local nonprofits or social service agencies, too, so they can include them in care packages sent to members of the community.

○ HELP PICK CROPS AT A LOCAL FARM

If you have a local farm in your area, it is probably a great resource for kid-friendly activities. One might be picking crops. Call ahead and see what they offer and how kids could be helpful. By teaming up with local farmers, you can provide your children with a screen-free activity that gets them outside, helps the community, and provides a tasty and nutritional snack to boot! Have your children wear old clothes they can get dirty. Supply each child with a pair of gloves and a hat. After receiving some instruction from the farm owner, let your kids pick strawberries, carrots, apples, or pumpkins ready for the season. Local orchards may also need help bagging products for customers or setting up baskets of crops to sell. With any luck, your kids may also get a juicy snack that is fresh from the fields.

○ VISIT A LONELY NEIGHBOR FOR A CHAT

If you are overwhelmed with the amount of chatter emanating from your kids, see if someone else might want to talk to them for a while. Start by getting to know your neighbors and identifying individuals or families who may be new to the area or not as familiar with other neighbors. Next, ask a new or lonely neighbor to come over for a chat with your children. Make this activity exciting by getting the neighbor's permission to be interviewed. Before the neighbor arrives, have your children compile lists of questions or things they want to know about this person. (Make sure that the questions are not too personal.) Make the interview session casual by offering snacks to share as your little ones and the neighbor chat it up at the kitchen table or on the back patio. After the visit, have each child write a story or draw a picture noting what they learned about this individual. Surprise the neighbor with a compilation of the pictures or stories in a folder or bind it together with yarn to serve as a keepsake.

◯ MAKE NO-SEW FLEECE BLANKETS FOR PROJECT LINUS

AGES 8–12
■■■

Project Linus is a nonprofit agency that donates blankets nationally to families in need. With just a little coordination, your kids can make several blankets in just a few hours. All you need is a bunch of fleece material and a few pairs of scissors to complete this project. Start by cutting fleece material into 4-foot squares. With fabric scissors, have older children cut out 4-inch sections from each corner. Next, prepare the edges of the blanket by cutting 4-inch strips from the outside of the blanket toward the inside all the way around. Once the strips are all cut, begin tying two strips together to create a knot and a fringe style. Travel all the way around the blanket until each strip is tied. And, voilà! The blanket is ready to deliver. Visit www.projectlinus.org to find blanket drop-off spots.

◯ HOST A BOOK EXCHANGE

AGES 6–12
■■☐

Show your kids how to share their love of reading by hosting a book exchange with their friends, family members, or neighbors. Before the gathering, ask each child to search through their rooms and bookshelves for stories they are willing to part with. Invite friends and family members to gather books they want to share, and set a time for a book exchange event. At the exchange, have everyone put their books on your kitchen table for others to browse. You can have each child choose a book to read or you can play a game that awards each kid with a random book. Let the bookworms take the books home to read and then plan a follow-up gathering to let them discuss the plotlines and stories they enjoyed. Make the event even more fun with book-themed decorations and snacks to share.

○ HOST A BABY ITEM COLLECTION

If your little ones are not so little anymore, show them how to eliminate the clutter in their rooms while donating gently used baby and kid items to a worthy cause. Cradles to Crayons is a nonprofit agency that connects with local families and agencies in need of baby items, toys, and clothing. Host your own drive by starting to collect items in your own home. Have the kids weed through their closets for gently used clothes and toys while you sort through those old tubs of baby clothes you were hanging onto. Get the word out, too, by having the kids contact their friends and family members, seeking donated items or cash to purchase baby supplies for families in need. Once you have a hearty collection, get in touch with Cradles to Crayons at www.cradlestocrayons.org to arrange a drop-off.

○ FORM A PARK LITTER TROOP

When you have a free day with nothing to do, devote it to improving the look of your community. Forming a park litter troop is more than just a way to give back to the community; it's also a way to teach your children not to litter. Make this cleanup activity a fun adventure by creating badges for your park litter troop. You can use fabric or construction paper to make each park ranger official. Then, give your kids protective gloves and trash bags. Send them into the park hunting for trash to remove from playgrounds, sidewalks, and open grassy areas. If you want to add a competitive touch to this activity, make a list of trash items each kid must find, such as soda cans, food wrappers, or water bottles so the cleanup crew can enjoy a scavenger hunt while beautifying the park.

○ COLLECT TOYS TO DONATE

It is likely that your children have an excess of toys, dolls, and teddy bears lying around their rooms. Teach them the importance of sharing with others while freeing your home of clutter. Local nonprofit organizations, hospitals, firefighters, and law enforcement agencies often come in contact with children who have lost toys and items they treasure due to a fire or natural disaster. A small toy can bring a smile to their faces or even offer them the comfort they need. Help your children become a part of these efforts by asking them to search through the playroom or their bedrooms for gently used dolls or teddy bears they can donate. While they don't have to give away their most treasured toy, when you explain how many children grow up without any toys, it may prompt them to gather even some of their favorite dolls and bears to help children in need. Bag up the dolls and bears and make arrangements to drop these off at hospitals or agencies for delivery to young children. You can also partner with Stuffed Animals for Emergencies. Learn more at https://stuffedanimalsforemergencies.org.

○ TAKE A FIRST AID WORKSHOP

If your children are interested in the medical field or need additional life skills to handle potential emergencies, enroll the entire family in a first aid workshop. Often times, local community centers or schools host these types of workshops. A typical first aid workshop covers potential emergencies that your children may encounter later in life. For example, the instructor may teach your family how to administer the Heimlich maneuver, bandage a cut, and detect signs of dehydration or allergic reactions. Have the kids take notes during the workshop so you can review the material once you get home. You can also have the kids help you compile a first-aid kit to keep at home or in your vehicle. Include bandages, antiseptic creams and ointments, and wet wipes.

○ PACK BACKPACKS FOR CHILDREN IN NEED

AGES 6-12
■□□

What kid doesn't like having a cool backpack filled with fun school supplies? Inquire with local elementary schools regarding the needs of children who might be coming to school without the supplies they need. Once you have a list of the supplies needed in your school district, search through your home for markers, glue sticks, kid-friendly scissors, pens, pencils, and notebooks, to donate. It's likely you also have a few gently used backpacks lying around that you can donate as well. If you are running low on supplies, ask family and friends for a few donations or head to the dollar store to pick up a few more items. Let your children take over the task of sorting through and dividing up the items while packing the bags. Encourage each kid to write a welcome letter for the child who receives each backpack or you can have them draw pictures to include.

○ HOST A STORYTIME SESSION

AGES 8-12
■■□

If your older children are avid readers, this activity is a perfect one. With an interested audience, they can share their favorite books and their reading skills with the younger generation. Prompt your kids to search through their book collections to find fun reading material appropriate for their younger siblings or the neighborhood children. Next, set up a time to host a storytime session to entertain the masses. Older children can read books to a group of young neighbors or you can make this activity even more interactive by preparing props, an impromptu puppet show to illustrate the plot, or even a souvenir from the book to distribute. Leave a lasting impression and a love for reading with the audience by making bookmarks to distribute as a parting gift after the storytime session.

○ DECORATE A FOOD COLLECTION BIN

Many organizations host food drives and place bins in community centers and retail stores. Your children can attract more attention to their efforts by decorating these collection bins to encourage more donations. Before letting your kids' artistic talents flourish, obtain permission from a nonprofit organization or pick up a bin to place in a store of your choice. Using colored construction paper or a roll of plastic tablecloth, have your children completely cover the bin. Tape the paper or plastic to the bin for a secure fit before decorating. Next, using markers, crayons, stickers, and glitter, add a festive look to the bin. Multiple children can decorate each side of the bin with their individual tastes or they can work together to color coordinate their art. If you have crepe paper, twist it around the opening of the food collection bin for additional flair. Once the colorful bin is ready, deliver it to the appropriate destination and watch as the donations pour in.

○ CREATE BIRDSEED ORNAMENTS

If you have bagels, peanut butter, and birdseed, you can decorate the outdoor areas of others' homes and provide nature's creatures with some nourishment. Turn those breakfast bagels into a unique ornament and fuel for neighborhood birds. Have each kid lay out bagels in halves on a paper towel in the kitchen. Then, using kid-friendly knives or even plastic silverware, spread peanut butter on the inside of each bagel half. Put bird seed on a plate and dip the bagel into the bird seed. Let the bagel dry and harden. Turn these bird treats into ornaments your friends and family can hang by stringing a piece of yarn or ribbon through the center hole of the bagel. Once the ornaments are ready, have your children surprise their loved ones with a gift that offers delight to both humans and flying creatures.

○ DELIVER BOTTLED WATER

Rising temperatures can pose health challenges to the men and women who work outside. Show your children the value of offering a simple gift to quench the thirsts of hardworking people by delivering water bottles on a hot summer day. Start by making a list of people in your neighborhood and community who could use a refreshing beverage in the middle of the day. Personnel such as garbage collectors, postal workers, construction workers, and law enforcement officials are often working in the trenches in the heat of the day. Then, gather coolers from your garage, fill them with water bottles, and add a layer of ice to keep the beverages ice cold. If you have some prepackaged single-serving snacks handy, toss these in a bag to deliver as well. Once the coolers are packed, head out into the community to spread goodwill and a refreshing treat to people hard at work. As a result, your children learn the value of staying hydrated while also gaining an appreciation of the efforts of those working for the community even when the temperatures continue to rise.

○ PAINT PLAYGROUND EQUIPMENT

Your kids probably spend hours on local playgrounds. Have them show their appreciation for the equipment they use by taking care of it! Contact your town's parks and recreation center or nearby daycares to see if you can paint or otherwise provide upkeep to any local spots. Older playground equipment often needs a paint touchup every few years, and playgrounds can be rife with weeds and trash. Plastic structures might benefit from a scrubbing with some Magic Erasers to clean minor graffiti or scratches. This is where your children can come to the rescue! Get the kids dressed in old clothes and pick up some paintbrushes, cleaning materials, and trash bags for a day of outdoor painting and cleaning.

○ SHOVEL A NEIGHBOR'S SIDEWALK AND DRIVEWAY

If your kids are bored with snowball fights but have extra energy to burn off, let them offer a helping hand to a neighbor. Snow shoveling is often strenuous work, so begin by fueling your kids with water and high-protein snacks to give them the energy they need. Next, instruct them on form so they are shoveling using the muscles in their legs versus just their backs to avoid any injuries. Make this activity a team effort by having one child draw a line with a stick to indicate the path to your neighbor's front porch or outline of the driveway. Then, let the shoveling begin. This activity doesn't have to be a serious one. Make it interesting by hosting a contest to see who can clear the largest portion of the sidewalk or driveway first. Add a little creativity to the project, too, by prompting the children to build a snowman to display in the front yard if it's okay with your neighbor.

○ HOST A LIFE SKILLS WORKSHOP

Even at a young age, your children have skills that they can share—whether it's braiding hair, throwing a curveball, or tying knots. Help them share these gifts with others. Invite some friends over for a life skills workshop. Set up stations that offer instructional, hands-on activities. For example, one station can include hair ties and a brush for braiding, and another can have rope for tying. Invite the guests to teach a skill they know as well. Let your children determine the skill they want to share and then give them the confidence they need to be the instructor for the day.

○ HUNT FOR LOOSE CHANGE TO DONATE

AGES 6-12

■□□

Your house probably has loose coins hiding out in pockets, couch cushions, and at the bottom of bags. Send your children on a scavenger hunt for loose change so they can surprise someone in need with a donation. Before you begin the hunt, make a list of charities of interest to your kids, whether it relates to animals, the environment, or education. Set a target goal for the amount of money you want to raise. Then, send your little ones off to hunt for loose change in the couch cushions, near the washer or dryer, or even on the floor of your vehicles. Your older kids probably have some change lying around in their rooms that they can add to the collection. Once the change is gathered, take the bags to a coin machine to get crisp dollar bills before dropping off the funds for a good cause.

○ MAKE PASTA BRACELETS FOR FRIENDS

AGES 6-12

■■□

Teach your children ways to value their friendships by launching this activity that helps them create a token of appreciation they can give away. Begin by setting out some dry pasta such as rigatoni, penne, or cannelloni noodles on your kitchen table. If you want to add some color to the bracelets, first place the pasta in a ziplock bag and add a squirt of hand sanitizer and food coloring, then shake to coat the pasta completely. Let the colored pasta dry while you cut strips of yarn based on the size of your kids' wrists. Make sure you cut the yarn a bit longer than needed to account for the tie. Next, have each child string the yarn through the noodles, using different types of pasta for variety. Leaving about an inch of the yarn exposed for a little leeway, wrap the bracelet around your child's wrist to complete the tie. The bracelet should fit loosely so your child can easily slip it off. When the bracelets are done, have your children present their friends with a token of their friendship.

○ PASS OUT PROGRAMS AT A LOCAL EVENT

Expose your children to some culture in your community while giving them the opportunity to help out local organizations. Many theater companies or community event organizers seek volunteers to pass out programs, and your children can gain a sense of belonging by offering their time and talents to a local event. To prepare for this volunteer opportunity, reach out to local organizations to inquire about events where greeters are needed. Local schools may need a few kids to open doors at play performances or sporting events. Your children could also help take tickets and guide visitors to a particular theater or ballroom at the community center. As an added bonus, after volunteering their time greeting guests and delivering programs, your kids may also get a chance to view the performance or participate in the event.

○ VOLUNTEER AT THE LIBRARY

Local libraries are often looking for "helpers" to stock shelves and tidy up the children's area. Get involved and encourage your kids to read at the same time when signing up for some volunteer time. Start by contacting your local library branch to determine their needs. For example, the library may need assistance hosting a storytelling event where your kids can serve refreshments or even try their hand at reading books to little ones. If the library is in need of books, prompt the kids to create a box for a book swap. With just a cardboard box or plastic bin, you can fill up the container with books you have lying around your home and then have the kids create flyers or signs to indicate that the books are free before placing it in the library lobby.

○ RUN A SOCCER CLINIC

If you have expert ball handlers in your household, encourage them to show off their talents and share their skills with others. Arrange for your tween to become the ultimate neighborhood soccer instructor for an hour by offering to teach children how to play. This activity is designed for older children and requires parental supervision for ultimate safety. Start by having your tween supply each child with a soccer ball. Then, have the "instructor" begin teaching each child how to dribble the ball. Help your child make the activity fun by having her teach the kids a game of follow the leader, where each child follows another child running in and out of cones while dribbling the ball. Once the team has learned how to handle the soccer ball, your child can stage a small scrimmage so the kids can showcase their talents. While it may take some time for the players to learn the tricks of the trade, your older child will feel good about lending her services while getting in some exercise.

○ DELIVER MEALS TO ELDERLY NEIGHBORS

It's likely that your family knows an elderly neighbor who has difficulty getting out and about. When cooped up in a house or apartment, it's challenging to try new foods or even dine out. Start by planning a meal option that your kids think an elderly neighbor would enjoy. Then, have them help you prepare the meal and package it in disposable plastic containers. Ask your children to personalize the package by making paper placemats and including a note about why this meal is particularly delicious. When the meal is ready, bring your kids along to deliver the goodies to show them how a small act can make a big difference in the lives of your neighbors.

○ BABYSIT FOR A FAMILY IN NEED

Let your older kids lend their services to local families by volunteering to babysit for free. Prepare your kids by teaching childcare skills, especially safety. (Many organizations such as YMCAs offer babysitting certification courses.) Begin by inquiring with parents (preferably of slightly older children, as opposed to infants) who need time to run errands without little ones and have your kids offer to babysit for an hour or two at a time. Pack a babysitting bag full of board games, small toys, books, coloring books, and crayons to make the visit much more entertaining. It is best for a parent or adult to be on call and nearby the first few times your child babysits to offer a sense of security to both the babysitter and the parents.

○ DECORATE PLACEMATS TO DONATE

While volunteering in soup kitchens and food pantries is appreciated, sometimes thinking outside of the box to provide others in need with something special makes even more of an impact. With just a few art supplies you probably have on hand, your children can make paper placemats that offer a burst of color and an encouraging message for diners. Break out stacks of white paper, construction paper, or cardstock to get started. Search for art supplies that will add even more creativity to this project, such as stickers, glitter glue, decals, and dry pasta. Have your children think about a design or theme and let them start decorating the pieces of paper. One child may choose to glue dry pasta along the edges of the paper to outline the placemat, while another may write encouraging messages such as "Have a great day" and "Enjoy your meal." Using markers or crayons, your kids can sign their first name to the placemat before delivering the stack to a local community center, nursing home, or soup kitchen.

○ MAKE A LIST OF GOOD DEEDS

AGES 6-12
■□□

When your children learn how small acts can benefit others, they may have more motivation to make a difference. If they brainstorm these acts themselves, the action will mean all the more. Give your kids a journal or pieces of paper for your brainstorming session and start with different categories to help them think of good deeds. For example, suggest good deeds that can be performed during the holiday season and then branch out to everyday deeds that are often appreciated by others. From collecting mail for a vacationing friend to carrying groceries in for an elderly neighbor, you may be surprised at the ingenious ideas your kids come up with. Once the list is complete, make a plan to perform at least one good deed every week.

○ CRAFT A THANKSGIVING CHAIN

AGES 6-12
■□□

The Thanksgiving season is the ideal time to help your children to count their blessings. With this fun-filled activity they can keep track of what they are thankful for and create a decoration to display at a holiday celebration. Start this project by cutting construction paper into strips. Have each child write down something or someone they are thankful for on the strip of paper and then make a link by stapling or gluing the ends of the strip together. The blessings may include names of family members and friends, privileges or talents your children appreciate, comforts they enjoy, or even an act of kindness someone performed for them at some point. As your children continue writing down their blessings, connect the links together to make a chain. Hang the Thanksgiving chain above your mantel, on the stairway, or set it out on your holiday table for all to see.

○ MAKE CARDS FOR THE HOMELESS

AGES 6-12

If you have saved birthday or holiday greeting cards, reuse these cards for an activity that can make others smile. Start by gathering a bunch of new and used greeting cards on your kitchen table and get the kids ready for an art project that will make a difference in the lives of the homeless, who are not accustomed to receiving mail. Using construction paper, crayons, markers, and the greeting cards, have your children make everyday greeting cards. They can use construction paper for the base of the card and then using kid-friendly scissors, cut up portions of other greeting cards to glue to the paper. Add stickers, illustrations, and inspiring messages to each card, such as "Wishing you well" or "Have a great day." Drop off these cards at a local shelter or outreach agency to be delivered.

○ HOST A WATER SPOT DURING A RACE

AGES 8-12

If your kids are active and seek out adventure, give them the chance to get right in the middle of the action by volunteering at a marathon or local race. Contact the race organizer to find out the best way to get involved and whether you need to supply the water and cups. Once you have approval to volunteer your services, set up tables at your designated mile marker of the race. Before and during the race, have each child fill up the water cups before the runners approach, then they can stand on the sidelines holding cups ready for the runners to grab. Make your water spot a welcoming one by having your children make signs or posters with encouraging messages such as "You're almost to the finish line" or "Keep going." Once the runners have passed their mark, let the cleanup begin. Make sure each child has a trash bag to pick up the water cups in the road or on the sidewalk and properly dispose of the trash before breaking down your water station.

○ MAKE A MAP OF YOUR NEIGHBORHOOD

AGES 8-12
■■■

Take your family's welcome wagon efforts to a creative level by prompting your children to create maps of your neighborhood for newcomers. Ideal for the entire family, this activity allows your kids to spotlight the highlights of your immediate vicinity. Give your children a map of the city to use as a reference point before you get started on this project. Then, supply them with blank pieces of paper, pencils, a ruler, and colored pencils or markers to add a decorative touch. Have each child draw straight lines using a ruler and a pencil and then label the names of the streets and nearby restaurants, stores, and schools. Add a bit of commentary to personalize the maps. For example, your child can create a legend to indicate the best places to eat, the houses with the most extensive holiday decorations, and the playgrounds with the best equipment. Once the maps are complete, make a family trip to a new neighbor's house to personally deliver the map.

○ RUN (OR WALK) A ROAD RACE

AGES 6-12
■■■

Let the runners in your family indulge in their need for speed while also supporting charities in your area. Many organizations host short runs and walks that your family can participate in each weekend. Visit websites of local organizations to find just the right event for your children. Local running stores commonly post information about races in the area too. Then, help the kids train for the big event. Stress the importance of hydrating and stretching before taking on a race or walk. Do some practice runs through the park or a nearby walking path to warm up their legs and test their endurance. Get the entire family involved and sign up to support the cause, too, even if you just plan to walk versus run. Many times races also encourage participants to raise additional funds by asking family members or neighbors to sponsor them.

○ EXERCISE FOR CHARITY

Show your children that exercise can be fun and that exercise with a purpose can help others. Get the kids moving and making money for their favorite charities. Start by helping your kids compile a grid sheet to collect donations. For example, they can ask family members, neighbors, and teachers to sponsor their next workout challenge and list specific goals they must reach on the grid sheet. From asking people to pledge a penny for each push up or jumping jack to requesting pledges for the number of minutes they can walk or ride a bike, your kids can get creative with how they raise funds while getting some exercise. Once the pledges are set, complete the exercise to see how much money they can raise while getting in shape. Bring along plenty of water to remain hydrated and make sure your children are supervised while working out for the day. Once the workout is over, add up the funds raised and donate it to a charity your children choose.

○ HELP A TEACHER SET UP A CLASSROOM

Show your kids the work that is involved with preparing for the school year with this activity designed for the week or two before school starts. Contact your local school district or a teacher who is a friend of the family to get your children immersed in setting up a classroom. Once you have scheduled a date and time to assist a teacher with classroom setup, cart the kids to the school to begin preparing the room and desks for new learners. With the guidance of a teacher, your kids can sharpen pencils, help tape signs to the walls, organize bookshelves, and make labels with students' names that adhere to desks or a bulletin board. If needed, bring along some school supplies to help out a teacher supply her students with the resources they need.

○ CRAFT PUZZLES FOR LOCAL PRESCHOOLS ■■□

AGES 8–12

Surprise small children at local preschools with a jigsaw puzzle that your kids can make from scratch. Gather up a large cardboard box, some spray adhesive, paper, and your creative kids to get this project going. With kid-friendly scissors, cut the cardboard box into a square shape. Have the kids draw an illustration on a white piece of paper, covering every space with color using crayons or markers. Next, glue the paper to the cardboard square. Once the paper dries, cover the paper with spray adhesive for your children. When the adhesive sets, have the kids use a pencil and draw puzzle shapes directly onto the paper. Help them cut out the puzzle pieces. Have your children try to put the puzzle back together to make sure all pieces fit before boxing up the pieces and donating the puzzle to a local preschool or daycare.

○ DECORATE LUNCH BOXES FOR SCHOOLS IN NEED

AGES 6–12

■■□

Lunch box designs are always a source of conversation among kids in school cafeterias. Your kids can help kids who are less fortunate feel good about their lunch box with this art project. Purchase a few plain-colored plastic lunch boxes from your local store and break out the art supplies in your home. Have the kids draw superhero logos, rainbows, or polka dots in permanent marker on the surface of the lunch boxes. You can also have them paint illustrations with acrylic paint and paintbrushes. Let the paint and marker dry before boxing up these lunch boxes to donate. If you don't have any plastic lunch boxes, consider having the kids decorate brown paper bags using crayons or markers. Drop off the colorful creations at your local school so they can disperse them to kids in need.

○ ATTEND A TOWN HALL MEETING

Guide your children through the process of how city governments operate while showing them ways to become informed citizens with this activity. Research the dates and times of town hall meetings in your area and load up the kids in the car to attend a community session that keeps them abreast of local issues and concerns. Prepare for the town hall meeting by discussing successes and challenges within your immediate area. For example, ask older children to identify any problems that they recognize while at school, in the community, or in their neighborhoods. Then, arm them with a notebook to take notes and head off to the town hall meeting. Have the kids jot down ideas or concerns they have while listening to city officials and residents speak at the meeting. Once you get home, talk about ways you and your family can promote positive change in your local area based on their notes.

○ LEARN SIGN LANGUAGE

Teach your kids how to expand their language and communication skills with this fun-filled activity. Take a trip to the library to check out books on sign language and then let the learning begin at home. Start by browsing through the library books on sign language to teach your kids simple signs. For example, learn how to sign words and phrases such as "please" or "thank you." While younger children may only be able to absorb just a few words or phrases each day, your older children can challenge themselves by learning how to sign complete sentences such as "How are you today?" If your local community center or college hosts workshops on sign language, sign the kids up for a formal lesson to advance their communication skills. You can also inquire with the city's office of disabilities to partner your children with deaf students so they can practice their skill and socialize at the same time.

○ MAKE MINI GREENHOUSES TO DONATE

AGES 6–12
■■□

Let your little green thumbs showcase their talent with this activity that encourages sharing the beauty of nature with others. With a few empty milk cartons, some soil, and seeds, show your kids how their efforts can bring color and life to neighbors and family members. First, cut off the top portion of a milk carton horizontally for your kids. Have your children fill the bottom portion of the carton with soil and then ask them to dig a small hole and plant flower seeds. Reattach the top part of the carton by taping the sides together and then add some water to the structure through the top opening. Instead of a carton, you can also use an oversized water bottle for your greenhouse. Next, accompany your kids to the homes of family members or neighbors to donate the mini greenhouse. Instruct the new owners of the greenhouse on how to water the plants and flowers to promote growth.

○ CRAFT CHESS BOARDS FOR RETIREMENT COMMUNITIES

AGES 8–12
■■□

Chess is a popular game for all ages. Help your children craft a chess board to donate to retirement communities with just a few steps and supplies you probably already have on hand. While many chess boards are made of wood or tile, you don't have to break out the heavy equipment or tools to create one with your kids. Instead, grab a plain piece of poster board for this activity. Start by having the kids draw a grid with sixty-four blocks using a black marker. Then, have them color in every other block with the black marker to resemble a chess board. Pick up a few playing pieces at the store on your way to a local nursing home or retirement community and then let the games begin. With permission from the centers, you can also have the residents teach your kids how to play the game using their newly created boards.

○ CLEAN UP COMMUNITY GRAFFITI

AGES 8-12

■■■

Graffiti-style murals can add color and life to structures. But, in some areas, graffiti is vandalism that can hinder the look of local buildings. With the permission of your city or business owners, help your older kids clean up the community. Dress the kids in old clothing and head out with large paintbrushes, rollers, and white paint. (Check with the city or a business owner to determine the color of paint they prefer if white is not an option.) Dip the paintbrushes in a paint tray filled with exterior paint and let the kids give the wall or building a fresh new look. While the kids can probably reach the lower areas of a structure, Mom and Dad will have to use a roller to hit the high spots.

○ CREATE A DRAWING FOR AN ART CONTEST

AGES 6-12

■■□

Your budding artist may need an outlet to showcase his talents and with this activity, he can also help support the community and inspire others. Many nonprofit agencies host art contests that may prompt your mini Picasso to put his work on display. Determine first the type of art your children want to create. From freehand illustrations and drawings to paintings stemming from watercolors or acrylic paint, the options are endless. Next, search for an art contest and determine the qualifications and guidelines. For instance, many contests stipulate a certain size for the artwork. The only thing left to do is supply your artists with the supplies they need, such as paints, paper, canvas plat-forms, markers, crayons, and glue. Once the masterpieces are ready to submit, plan to spend some time browsing through the other work on display to admire the talents of the youth in your community and inspire your children to continue sharing their talents.

○ WASH NEIGHBORHOOD DOGS

The dog lovers in your family can share their time and talents while surrounding themselves with furry friends when hosting this wet but fun activity. With just a few supplies, such as dog shampoo, large containers, and a hose, your kids can clean up the family pet and the neighborhood dogs to support the community. An adult should first inquire with family members or neighbors regarding their need for pet cleanings. Then, schedule a time to bring the dogs to your garage or yard for a wash. With adult supervision, let the kids put each dog into a large, spacious bucket or container and then begin rinsing them off with the hose. One child may need to hold the dog's body or leash while the other scrubs down the canine companion. Thoroughly dry off the dog with a towel and return him to his owner smelling fresh and clean.

○ MAKE MEDALS FOR CHILDREN

Everyone should feel appreciated at some point, and with this activity you have the opportunity to show your children how many ways there are to appreciate others. With just a few household items you can craft medals for your children to reward others with when they need it the most. Start by cutting small circles from a cardboard box to serve as the medals. Then, have your children glue construction paper around the cardboard and decorate the medal with crayons or markers. Punch a hole in the top of the medal and string through a piece of yarn to create a necklace. Then, brainstorm with the kids about ways to reward others. For example, if they see a friend help someone in need, they can present him with a medal for sharing goodwill. Keep these on hand so your children can distribute them when they witness a good deed.

○ PLAN A COMMUNITY GAME NIGHT

Prompt your kids to meet new people by planning a community game night. Contact the community center or your local YMCA to offer your family's services in organizing this fun-filled activity. Once you have permission to host a game night, have your kids help get the word out by creating fliers to hang in local stores or at the park, and have an adult spread the word on social media. Then, start planning by gathering board games that are popular, such as checkers, chess, Monopoly, and kids' Trivial Pursuit. On the day of the event, set up tables and chairs for each game and instruct your kids to welcome guests as they enter, showing them the game options. You can also make snacks and have the kids help you make lemonade and cookies to serve during the game night.

○ HOST A TOY EXCHANGE

It's likely that your kids have toys that they don't use often—and their friends probably do too. But one kid's boring toy is another kid's treasure! Have some fun while spreading goodwill with a toy swap that emphasizes sharing. Invite over a few of your kids' friends and instruct each one to bring a toy or two they'd like to swap. Then, while gathered in a circle, have each child describe the toy she brought for the party. Next, have each child pass his toy to the right and give the kids a chance to explore the toy and play for a few minutes. Have the kids reconvene into the circle and ask them to pass to the right again. Continue the process of passing and playing until each child has had a chance to see all the toys firsthand. Then, host a drawing to see who gets to keep each toy. For example, put all the kids' names in a hat and draw out a name for each toy. If they want to swap after the drawing, then let the bargaining begin.

○ COLLECT ITEMS FOR FIRE VICTIMS

AGES 8-12
■■□

Devastation from losing all of your belongings in a fire is hard to fathom. Show your children how to help others recover with this activity designed to supply fire victims with essential household items as they rebuild their lives. Start by making a list of general items people may need, such as hygiene products, paper towels, toilet paper, basic clothing items, and kitchen utensils. Then, while accompanied by an adult, send your children out into the neighborhood to request donations of items or money to purchase the items. You can also have the kids contact family members or friends for assistance. If you like, expand your efforts into the school or community by posting signs soliciting donations and spreading the word on social media. Once you have gathered all the items, drop them off with a local agency that supports fire victims. If you personally know a family in need and living in temporary housing, you and the kids can deliver the items yourselves.

○ SPONSOR A FAMILY GARAGE SALE

AGES 6-12
■■□

Get your home free of clutter and raise some funds for a worthy cause by having your kids help you pull off a family garage sale. After choosing a local charity to benefit from the sale, send your kids into their rooms and the playroom to gather gently used toys and clothing. Set up tables in your garage or driveway and have the kids make pricing signs. For example, have one table where all the goods are fifty cents, one for $1 items, and another for items that are $5. Distribute the items on the tables and assign each kid a table to work during the garage sale. While younger children may need some help making change, older children can guide them and even help bag up items at the sale. Once the sale is over, tally up the money and donate it to a charity.

○ PLAN A NEIGHBORHOOD BLOCK PARTY

If you are new to the area or haven't had a chance to get to know the neighbors, help the kids plan a neighborhood block party to meet everyone in a casual setting. The first thing you and the kids need to do is set a date, time, and location for the party. Then, ask the kids to create fliers noting the details of the party. With an adult's assistance, the children can deliver the invitations to each mailbox. Next, begin planning activities and refreshments. You and the kids can make some cookies, punch, or appetizers for the event. Make sure you also plan a few games so the neighbors can get to know each other while having fun. Break out the board games when hosting the party indoors or toss some jump ropes, Hula-Hoops, or soccer balls into the backyard for an outdoor gala.

○ MAKE A WREATH FOR NEW NEIGHBORS

Welcome new families into the neighborhood while giving your children a chance to express their creativity with this activity. Although this art project may require a trip to the craft store, the end result is sure to delight and impress those new faces on the block. Gather paper towels, twine, kid-friendly scissors, ribbon, and dry reeds (you can find these in the silk flower area of a local craft store). Start by having your kids place the reeds in a tub of warm water to soak for about thirty minutes. Let each child dry the reeds with a paper towel and then show them how to gently bend them to form a circle. Then, use the twine to tie the reeds together 4 inches apart. Once the reeds are dry, the creativity begins. Tie ribbons onto the wreath or add dried flowers for a festive look appropriate for the season. Once the wreath is complete, take a trip to the neighbors' house to deliver the welcoming gift.

○ CRAFT DREAM CATCHERS FOR A COMMUNITY CENTER

AGES 8-12

■■□

If your local community center is starting to look drab, get the kids excited about decorating it with this art project they can personalize, deliver, and admire each time you visit the center. To start making a dream catcher to donate, you'll need a plastic coffee can lid, a hole punch, kid-friendly scissors, yarn, and double-sided tape. You may also want to add decorative touches such as beads or feathers. Start by helping the kids cut the center out of the lid so just a 1-inch rim is left. With the hole punch, punch a hole in the rim so you can tie a piece of yarn that serves as the hanging structure. Then, attach the double-sided tape around the rim. Cover the lid with yarn for a decorative look and then wrap pieces of yarn across the center of the lid. Have the kids string beads to yarn or attach feathers to the rim of the lid to personalize the dream catcher. All that's left to do is deliver the colorful dream catcher and hang it in the community center.

○ HOST A NEIGHBORHOOD PET SHOW

AGES 6-12

■■□

If your neighborhood is full of pets of all shapes and sizes, try hosting a neighborhood pet show. To begin organizing this activity, have an adult contact neighbors who have pets to inquire about a day or time to host the show. Then, once all the neighbors and pets are onboard, set up an area in your front or backyard for all to gather, including the pups, kittens, and small creatures in cages. Make sure all animals are on leashes and separated from one another, and once all guests have arrived, have each child showcase his or her pet. You can also have them demonstrate commands or tricks to further delight the audience. Have each child share something special or unique about his or her pet, too, for added entertainment.

○ CRAFT DUCT TAPE WALLETS FOR SHELTERS

AGES 8–12

■■■

Help your kids supply the wallets for people to store their personal identification with this art project. Begin this project by cutting four 10-inch strips of duct tape and placing them on a table with the adhesive side upright. Layer the strips of duct tape so they attach on the horizontal edges. Make another set of four strips and layer them as well. Stick the two sets of duct tape together, attaching the adhesive sides. Trim the sheet of duct tape so it is about 9 inches wide and fold the structure in half. Tape together one side of the wallet to create a pocket and then fold the wallet to the left to complete the project. Make this art project a little more colorful by intertwining different-colored strips of duct tape.

○ HOST A FAMILY FACE-OFF

AGES 6–12

■□□

Spend some time getting to know the families in your neighborhood with a family face-off event. If there is a new family who has just moved into the neighborhood or a new child who's enrolled in your kids' school, then take the opportunity to host a family game night at your home to show your kids how to befriend others and offer a welcoming environment. This interactive game showcases just how much you know about your family members. Have each family member write out a question, such as "Who has the cleanest room?" or "Who likes avocados?" Then, the person who wrote the question gets to play the host while the family playing the game tries to come to an agreement on how to answer the question. If the family comes up with the correct answer, they get a point. Then, move on to the next family for a round of this guessing game. The family with the most points at the end of the game wins.

○ SHARE MUSICAL TALENTS WITH RETIREMENT COMMUNITIES

AGES 8-12

Your musically inclined kids can share their talents by hosting a performance at a local retirement home. Pack up their instruments, such as small keyboards, trumpets, flutes, or even harmonicas to entertain the community. Once you arrive at the retirement home, have each child play a song they know. Even something as simple as "Twinkle, Twinkle, Little Star" offers the residents entertainment for a few minutes. If your children have mastered their instrument, they can even take requests from the audience. Many retirement homes also have a piano onsite the kids can play. Host a sing-along, too, to get the residents active in the performance.

○ HOST AN EMERGENCY TRAINING DRILL

AGES 6-12

Your kids probably practice emergency drills at school, but have you done the same thing at home? While you don't want to scare kids, you want the peace of mind knowing that they know what to do in such an unfortunate event. To host an emergency training drill, spend time discussing ways to respond to a fire, earthquake, or tornado. For example, during a tornado, your children should find shelter in areas of the home that are away from windows. During a fire, they should know how to assess heat on doorknobs and stop, drop, and roll. An earthquake should prompt the kids to drop, cover, and hold on to a sturdy structure away from windows until the shaking stops. You can also plan a well-known and safe local meeting spot if for some reason family members get separated from one another. Be sure kids have memorized parents' cell phone numbers. Once you've informed your kids of the actions to take, help them host a drill for each type of emergency.

○ CREATE A PENNY DRIVE

■□□

Pennies have become almost a throwaway coin—but when you put a bunch together, they really add up to a lot of money! Once your children have chosen a charity, talk about how every cent counts. Have them start by searching their rooms and your home for pennies. Next, take your fundraising efforts to the street. Walk with your children to homes of trusted neighbors or family members and have them explain that they are collecting pennies for a particular charity. You can even decorate old coffee cans or paper bags to house the pennies. Once the collection is complete, take the pennies to a local bank to convert the change into dollar bills before donating the money.

○ TAKE A NEW STUDENT ON A CITY TOUR

■■□

Help your kids see the value of welcoming someone new to your city by partnering with the school to greet a new student. After coordinating with the principal, your child's teacher, and his or her parents, set up a few hours for you and the kids to give this new student a tour of the city. Before the big day, help the kids set up an itinerary for your excursion. If you are taking a walking tour, think about the sights in your neighborhood such as a local park, fishing area, or playground. If you plan to take a driving tour, ask your children to write down a few kid-friendly hotspots in your city, such as water parks, cool monuments or sculptures, restaurants, or toy stores. Then, set out for the day. Take plenty of pictures and have your children create a scrapbook for the new student so he or she can refer back to the tour while getting familiar with the city.

○ CALL A LONG-DISTANCE RELATIVE

AGES 6–12

■□□□

With texting and emailing, many kids aren't learning the art of a polite phone call. Teach them those skills while also brightening a relative's day. Before dialing the number of a relative, come up with a list of topics to discuss. For example, your child may want to tell an aunt about a school project he is working on or ask a grandparent for advice on how to sew a button or fix a toy. Prompt your kids to think about exciting events within the past few weeks that they could describe to a relative or even brag a little about their accomplishments at school or at sporting events. Make a cheat sheet for your child to refer to during the phone call. Then, before making the call, offer reminders about polite ways to address people on the telephone, such as saying "yes" instead of "yeah" and "please" and "thank you."

○ READ BOOKS AT HOSPITALS

AGES 8–12

■■□

It's easy for bedridden hospital patients to get bored. Some may even have headaches that make it hard to read or watch TV. With this activity, your children can help ease the pain and eliminate boredom for patients and for themselves. Start by contacting a local hospital or children's hospital in the area to inquire about volunteer opportunities. Let the coordinator know that your children would like to read books to patients. Once you have approval to venture into the hospital, have your kids select a few of their favorite books and head out for this volunteer opportunity. Lead your children into the rooms of patients who have agreed to have visitors read to them and watch as your kids brighten someone else's day.

○ LAUNCH AN ICE PATROL

Winter storms can wreak havoc on driveways and sidewalks, making it unsafe for many elderly residents to exit their home. Your kids can help when bundling up to brave the cold and forming an ice patrol. Dress warmly, then fill up small buckets with ice salt or sand. Reduce the risk of harm or injury by cautioning your children about how to navigate ice and slick spots on the road or sidewalks. Load the ice patrol supplies, complete with a few shovels or plastic cups, in a wagon or wheelbarrow and begin making your way through the neighborhood with your children, spreading salt or sand on slick areas. (Make sure that you obtain permission from each resident before applying the materials.) What your kids may find is that the appreciation warms their hearts in even the most frigid temperatures.

○ JOIN IN A SECRET SANTA PROGRAM

Bring the magic of the holiday season into the hearts of your kids when helping them participate in a Secret Santa program. Show them how their gently used toys can make a difference in the lives of children who may not have any presents to open on Christmas Day. While you contact local shelters, Boys & Girls Clubs, Toys for Tots, or YMCA facilities to inquire about how to donate toys for children, the kids can begin scouring through their rooms for gently used toys. Using a wet cloth and some soap, have your kids spot-clean the toys you'll donate. Next, help your kids wrap each toy in a box and add a bow so the package is just as pretty as the gift. Your children can also add inspiring messages to the gift tag, such as "Have a wonderful holiday" or "You are special." Some organizations prefer to get new, unwrapped toys—be sure to check ahead of time.

○ GET INVOLVED IN THE VOTING PROCESS

AGES 8–12
■■■

When election time rolls around, help your kids become informed citizens by getting them involved in the voting process. Before election day, make a list of the candidates in local and national races. In age-appropriate ways, discuss the issues that each candidate has put forth a position on and get your kids' opinions on who to vote for in each race. They might find local issues easier to understand—such as how to develop land in your area or how to allocate the town's budget money. Then, when voting day arrives, take them with you to the polls so they can see how voting works. When you get home, let the kids vote themselves by creating small ballot boxes. Each child can write down who he or she wants to vote for on a small slip of paper and put it in the ballot box designated for each race. Tally up the results to determine the winners.

○ CARRY GROCERY BAGS AT THE STORE

AGES 8–12
■■□

When the kids are bored and you need a few items from the store, bring them along and show them how to give back to others while flexing their muscles. After your shopping trip is complete, load up your own groceries and then station the kids outside of the store for a few minutes to offer their assistance. Remain with them to ensure their safety and show them how to approach people with multiple bags or full shopping carts and offer to help haul groceries and load them into vehicles. Your children may find that just one tiny gesture reinforces the good in the world and shows others that a helping hand is always available.

○ TACKLE FOOD WASTE

Have you ever noticed the food that gets wasted when your family goes out to eat? Let this experience launch into an activity that helps feed those in your community who are hungry. Talk to your kids about food waste and how you can adjust habits in your own home to avoid it. Then consider educating local restaurant owners on how to donate excess food to local pantries and shelters. Start by investigating local or national programs that coordinate these services, such as Rescuing Leftover Cuisine (www.rescuingleftovercuisine.org), MealConnect (www.mealconnect.org), or Replate (www.re-plate.org). Next, stop in at local delis or restaurants and discuss ways that the owners can help feed the hungry with leftover food from the day. Ideal for older children, this activity helps your kids to see the devastating effects of hunger while also prompting them to take action for a worthy cause.

○ SCRAPBOOK FOR A FAMILY MEMBER

Kids love to see old photos of themselves and family members. Preserve these memories and offer a priceless gift to relatives with this activity. Break out your box of old family pictures and have your children choose some of their favorite photos. Then, create a scrapbook for a designated family member, such as an aunt or grandparent. While you can use blank photo albums or scrapbooks purchased from the store for this activity, you can also create a book with construction paper and yarn that you have on hand. Have each child glue or tape photos onto the construction paper pages and label the images or write comments to share. Once the pages are dry and ready to assemble, hole punch the pages and tie them together with small pieces of yarn. Your children can also make a cover page for the scrapbook and write a note to the family member before dropping off a present that keeps the family memories alive.

○ START A ROUND ROBIN CHAIN LETTER

AGES 8–12
■■□

As a kid, it's always exciting to receive mail. However, in this electronic age, snail mail is much less prominent. Get your kids excited about walking to the mailbox with this activity that also delivers a surprise to the mailbox of your family members. For this activity designed for older kids, the object is to create a round robin chain letter that keeps them in touch with long-distance relatives and cousins. Begin by brainstorming family members who live far away and then have your children write letters detailing what's new with their daily activities, schoolwork, and athletic events. Once the letter is finished, add a list of other relatives who have agreed to be a part of the chain letter for the recipient to send a letter to next, with their information at the bottom of the list. Within a few weeks, your children should begin checking the mailbox to read the responses.

○ TAKE DOG TREATS TO THE DOG PARK

AGES 6–12
■□□

Whether you have a dog to take to the local dog park or your kids just want to play with the neighborhood dogs, you and your children can show goodwill to furry friends since they are part of the community too! Before heading out to the dog park, pack up some healthy dog treats in plastic bags. Give each child a bag of treats to distribute at the park. Before approaching animals, though, make sure you have the owner's permission to distribute treats and guidance on how to approach his or her pets. In order to avoid overfeeding man's best friend, offer to leave the bag of dog treats with dog owners once you leave the park. A simple gesture toward someone's beloved pet is just one additional way you can show your children how to be kind when people least expect it.

○ COMPLIMENT A STRANGER

Good deeds don't have to be extravagant gestures. In fact, your children can make someone smile just by vocalizing their observations. While it is not always safe to encourage your children to approach strangers, you can teach them how to compliment others with your supervision and common-sense guidance. For example, you can say that you like the grocery store cashier's hair or express how well behaved a pet is while on a morning walk. Ask your kids to think about compliments that would make others feel good about themselves and let them give it a try.

○ COLLECT USED BOOKS FOR AFTER-SCHOOL PROGRAMS

Many after-school programs are in need of supplies and instructional materials. Your kids can make a difference in the community by sup-plying these programs with the educational materials they need if you host a used-book drive. Get the word out by having your children make fliers advertising their efforts and having an adult make rele-vant posts on social media. Use construction paper and bright colors to capture attention, and hang these signs in your neighborhood and community centers with a contact number for an adult supervising the project. You could use your porch as a drop-off spot, or tell your neighbors that you'll come door to door in a specified time window to pick up their donations. Make sure you bring along a wagon to transport the reading material! You and your kids can also inquire with the local library to see if they have any leftover donations to contribute. Once you've collected a hefty set of books, box up the supplies and head to the nearest YMCA or after-school program to drop off the old books, while feeling good about providing young children with knowledge and entertainment.

○ MAKE A WALL OF ART

If your refrigerator is overrun with colorful masterpieces, share the wealth with your community! Just gather up some art supplies, paper, and tape to launch this creative project. As your children are making even more illustrations or coloring pages from a coloring book, contact your local community center to see if they could use some colorful creations for their hallway walls. Once you have permission, have the kids determine a theme for their artwork. For example, you could create a holiday-themed wall for Halloween and have the kids illustrate ghosts and goblins to hang on the wall. Make multiple pages to fill a large space and then head to the community center to hang the creations.

○ ADOPT A FAMILY FOR THE HOLIDAYS

If your children are unsure how to give back when the holidays roll around, this activity is perfect for them, especially when they see just how much their efforts impact holiday celebrations for families unable to purchase presents for their children. To adopt a needy family in your community, start by contacting local churches or a social service agency to identify a family in need. You can also contact organizations such as Soldiers' Angels for a referral at www.soldiersangels.org. The organizations provide a list of the family members, complete with ages of the children, clothing sizes, and toy preferences. With the list in hand, head to the store to fill your carts with items for the family. Toss in a few household or hygiene items, too. Have the kids wrap each present and make a card for the recipients before dropping off the items for the organization to deliver.

◯ TEACH MUSIC LESSONS

■■■

If you have a musical genius in your crew, show your child how to share his or her talents by offering music lessons for friends, family members, or young neighbors. Break out the instruments—from kazoos and small drums to flutes and trumpets—to launch a group musical lesson that is bound to fill your home with tunes. Pair off each child with a partner who has never played a chosen instrument and let them spend a few minutes instructing how to play. Even if your children just know how to play a few notes, they can share a bit of musical enjoyment with another child, hopefully prompting a love for music. Let the dancers in your crew share their talents, too, with an instructional session in the living room. Once the lessons are complete, host a talent show so each kid can show off his or her newfound talent.

◯ WRITE AN APPRECIATION LETTER TO AN ARTIST OR AUTHOR

■■☐

Your little bookworms probably have a favorite book or author that they turn to when it's time to read. Let them express their appreciation for these fun-filled words by writing appreciation letters to local authors or artists. Before breaking out the stationery, ask your kids to choose their favorite book. While gathered at a table, look through the books to identify the author and the illustrator. With your help, the kids can see if the author has a website with contact information. If not, look up the publishing company's address. Then, supply each child with a thank you note, piece of stationery, or a blank piece of paper. Instruct each child to write the author or artist of the book, expressing what they loved the most about the pictures or the storyline. Fold the letters into envelopes and show the kids how to address them and add a stamp before heading to the mailbox to send off these fan letters.

○ LEARN HOW TO RAISE AND FOLD A FLAG

AGES 8-12
■■■

Your kids have probably seen flags flying at their school and all over town (maybe even on your own house), but do they know how to take care of one? If you're not sure yourself, contact your local veteran's organization and set out for a day of learning how to raise and fold a flag. Partner your children with a few veterans and have them take part in an informal ceremony to raise the flag on a flagpole. Then, ask the veterans to show them the proper way to fold a flag. You can even purchase a flag prior to your visit and then donate it to the organization as a way to support the community.

○ PUBLISH A NEIGHBORHOOD NEWSPAPER

AGES 10-12
■■■

Share your neighbors' good news by helping your children create a neighborhood newspaper. On a nice day when lots of neighbors are socializing outside, provide each child with a notebook and a pen and send them off to interview neighbors you trust to gather the latest news. Prompt them to ask questions about accomplishments, occupations, family activities, and more so the newspaper offers a wide variety of news your neighbors can enjoy. Once your children return with the information they gathered, have them begin writing stories and creating drawings that reveal what they learned from each neighbor. You can even have them write down upcoming activities within the community that families may enjoy, such as picnics, festivals, or other local events. Once they have finished each page, make copies of the newspaper and bind them together using a three-hole punch and yarn. All that's left to do is distribute the news to the neighbors.

4. PUT A FUN TWIST ON LOCAL TRAVEL

When you take vacations to faraway places, you probably spend time planning activities for your kids to do. It's those short trips—to the doctor's office, to a local restaurant, to Grandma's house—when your kids can quickly get bored. Minimize the frustration that stems from hungry bellies while waiting for your food to arrive at a restaurant with a sugar packet game or blindfolded tasting party. Teach your children how to speak Pig Latin on your morning walk. Boost their excitement while camping in the woods or after swimming near the beach with these screen-free activities designed to help them collaborate and host healthy competitions with their friends and siblings. From educational road trip games that challenge your kids to count or observe cars driving by to sharing games that reveal family secrets, thoughts, and feelings, these one hundred activities give you and your children plenty to do while out and about.

○ PLAY I SPY AT THE ZOO

Even though the zoo is usually entertainment enough, sometimes you have to walk awhile from one spot to another or wait for a show to start. If so, entertain the kids with a classic game of I Spy. Have one child find a "thing," say something like "I spy something blue" or "I spy something round" and then encourage the rest of your troop of kids to begin guessing the object. Make the game competitive with older children by tallying up points for each correct guess or promise a sweet treat for the one who guesses in the least amount of time. Especially in outdoor areas, the sky is literally the limit when choosing objects to "spy."

○ LAUNCH A NEIGHBORHOOD SCAVENGER HUNT

If you are enjoying a staycation, give your kids an adventure with a neighborhood scavenger hunt. Even better, you can customize this activity to accommodate the ages of your children and the nature of your neighborhood. For example, if you have little ones, have them brainstorm household items they could collect from very familiar neighbors, such as a napkin, a piece of fruit, or a red pen. Give older kids a challenge with items on the list such as a blooming red rose or a paper clip. Once the lists are complete for all age groups, have an adult contact the neighbors you'll be approaching to get their buy-in. Then discuss how to approach each neighbor. The only thing left to do is pair off your children and venture out into the neighborhood with them to find the items. The first team to return home with everything on the list wins.

○ CREATE CRAZY BOWLING MOVES

It may be hard to believe, but even a visit to the bowling alley can bore children while they are waiting for their turn to knock down the pins. Put a little pizazz into the game by creating a game of crazy bowl. Try out some of these moves to ramp up the fun at the bowling alley: Challenge each child to bowl one round with her eyes closed, bowl with her nondominant hand, roll the ball through someone else's legs, or bowl in slow motion. Your kids can also sit on the floor and roll the ball by pushing it with their feet, bowl backward, or spin around three times before rolling the ball down the lane. You can add on bonus points for tricks or follow the traditional scoring model when playing crazy bowl, but regardless of the method, the winner of the game has earned some credibility for her skills.

○ TRY A NEW DISH AT A RESTAURANT

If your children are tired of eating the same selections or resist trying new things, give this activity a shot. Scour through the menu and find a new, unique appetizer or small meal that everyone can take a few bites of before their main dish. If you want to add more excitement to this activity, order a sampler plate and see who will try the most items. Award points or even a dessert to the child who tries the most "new" foods.

○ LEARN TO ROLLER SKATE BACKWARD

AGES 8-12

Designed for older children, this challenge offers a test of their skills, balance, and willingness to try something new. Once your tweens have mastered the art of skating forward, teach them a new method to circle the rink backward. Have each skater begin by positioning the heels out and the toes inward while keeping the back straight and the knees bent. Have each skater slowly lift his knees in this position while keeping skates in the original foot position. Once they get the hang of it and feel balanced, have them slowly apply more force and begin to push themselves backward while lifting the knees slightly with each push. While it may take a few falls to get the hang of it, before long, your kids will be sailing backward around the rink.

○ PLAY *THE PRICE IS RIGHT* AT THE GROCERY STORE

AGES 8-12

A routine trip to the grocery store doesn't have to leave you feeling frustrated as your kids beg for every item on the shelf. Instead, turn this trip into a game and a math lesson at the same time by playing *The Price Is Right*. The goal is for your kids to guess as close to the actual price of selected items on the shelves. Begin the game by appointing one child as the host of the game. The host is responsible for finding one food item on the shelves and writing down the price of the item where the other children cannot see. Each child in your group gets a chance to guess the price and the closest guess wins. Keep this game going through each aisle of the grocery store where each child gets a chance to be the host of the game. Or, play it while you wait in line to check out with the food in your cart. You can tally up points for the winner and then that child gets to choose one treat from the store to share with the rest of the players.

○ LOCATE BIRDS AT THE PARK

Turn your kids into master birdwatchers when visiting the city park. Set a large blanket down in a grassy area, then have each child lie down and start pointing out birds or groups of birds. See if they can name the types of birds, such as red cardinals, sparrows, hawks, hummingbirds, blue jays, and blackbirds. If you have a pair of binoculars handy, let the kids take turns getting a closer look. Turn this bird-watching journey into a game by having your children write down the types of birds they see or see how many birds in a cluster they can count.

○ WRITE A VACATION WISH LIST

A vacation wish list is similar to a bucket list and can give your kids a goal to work toward as they pass the time on a vacation. While you can easily just sit your children down at the table and supply them with paper and pens to make a list, mix it up a little and have them create a vacation wish list booklet. For example, your daughter may want to swim with the dolphins in Florida whereas your son may want to go to a luau in Hawaii. If you have journals or sketchbooks on hand, use these or once the list is complete, you can always punch holes in the sides and tie together the wish list books with yarn or ribbon. Encourage your children to get creative by making one page for each destination and sketching out an activity they would like to participate in once there.

○ PLAY "HOW MANY CAN YOU NAME?" IN THE CAR

■■☐

If your kids are getting antsy in the back seat and I Spy or the ABC game is not keeping them occupied, it might be time to play the "How Many Can You Name?" game. All you need is a stopwatch! Before you start, have the kids brainstorm a list of common items or things that could serve as categories, such as colors, cartoon characters, teachers, or even names that begin with a particular letter. Write the categories on strips of paper and put them in a ball cap or container in your car. When it is time to begin, have the child choose a category out of a hat and announce it. The timekeeper should start the stopwatch and the player must name as many items in the category within thirty seconds. Repeat the process by having the next child choose a category and begin naming items. The player who names the most wins.

○ HOST A SCAVENGER HUNT AT THE MALL ■■☐

Turn a routine shopping trip into an adventure when taking your kids to the mall. Instead of battling the cries of "I want this," watch as your children scope and scour through the stores seeking out items on a list with this scavenger hunt. Before heading to the mall, make a list of items your children must "spy" while you are browsing the aisles. For example, you could include household items such as a bottle of blue cleaning solution, a bright red piece of clothing, or a popular type of sneaker. Brainstorm items in stores you plan to frequent, such as appliances, electronics, or shoes to include on the scavenger hunt list. Make a list with different items for each child or form teams to add a competitive edge to this activity. The first child or team to find every item on the list wins.

○ MAKE NEWSPAPER HATS TO TOUR MEDIA OUTLETS

Put a new twist on your next field trip to tour a media outlet by out-fitting your children in appropriate attire. After scheduling a tour to the local TV station, radio outlet, newsroom, or printing press, prepare for the adventure by making newspaper hats. Before crafting the hats, spend some time learning about what is happening in the community by reading through the newspaper. From sports to local town news, this activity gives your kids a chance to learn what's going on around them. Gather a piece of old newspaper and fold the top corner of the newspaper into the center of the newspaper and then fold the bottom corner of the newspaper into the center to form a triangular shape. Fold up the bottom of the hat 2 inches toward the center and then seal all sides of the paper with tape. Turn the hat over and open from the center before placing it on your child's head to complement his wardrobe for the field trip.

○ HOST A BLINDFOLDED TASTING PARTY

Entertain your kids while dining out with a blindfolded tasting party that is sure to bring giggles to the table. Simply slip a bandana or handkerchief in your purse or travel bag before heading out. Once the food arrives at your table, select one child to wear the blindfold and place a variety of food from each person's plate on one plate in front of the first player. (Finger foods work best for a tasting party.) Next, have the child try a bite of the food and try to guess what he or she is eating. Keep tally of how many food items he or she guesses correctly. Take turns having each child join the tasting party while blindfolded.

⭘ PLAY A ROAD TRIP GUESSING GAME

Entertain kids of all ages during car rides with a road trip guessing game. With a little preparation and a few odd objects gathered before you leave, you can keep them guessing for hours while playing this game. All you need is a few paper bags and some interesting objects to pack up before hitting the road. Give your children paper bags and have them search your home for small items such as toys, cotton balls, straws, pens, and plastic utensils. Be sure they don't show each other what's inside their bags! Roll up the bags and pack them in the car to pull out when cries of "Are we there yet?" start to surface. Then, your children can swap bags and reach into them one at a time with their eyes closed to see if they can guess the objects.

⭘ CREATE A HOTEL ROOM OBSTACLE COURSE

When cramming a family into a hotel room, the close quarters are bound to cause some frustration—especially if you are facing a rainy afternoon. Turn those frowns upside down with a hotel room obstacle course that prompts your kids to get creative. Using items you typically find in a hotel room, construct barriers with your children that can serve as an interactive course. For example, you can lay down sofa cushions or pillows on the floor to hop or skip over, tie a sheet to two chairs for a makeshift limbo pole, or balance books or brochures on heads while walking the perimeter of the room. Set up the rules of the obstacle course before the competition begins and then time each child as they navigate through the close quarters. This activity requires adult supervision to avoid any injuries or damage to the hotel room.

◯ PLAY "DON'T STEP ON A CRACK"

■ ☐ ☐

Turn a leisurely walk into an obstacle course when playing "Don't Step on a Crack" with your children. Because this game stems from a popular nursery rhyme, you can test your kids' coordination skills and their musical talents all at once. The nursery rhyme goes, "Don't step on a crack or you'll break your mother's back." Start by lining up each child at the start of a crack in the sidewalk before taking a walk throughout the neighborhood. Next, instruct each child that the goal is to avoid all cracks in the sidewalk. And, if they do step on one, they are out of the game until the next round. As an added bonus, you can moan and groan while holding your pretend backache each time they step on a crack. Entertain the little ones during this game by singing the nursery rhyme or prompting them to skip, jump, hop, or trot at certain times during the walk, all while avoiding the cracks.

◯ PLAY A ROAD TRIP ABC GAME

■ ■ ☐

Even if you're not driving far, sometimes traffic can turn a twenty-minute drive into an hour-long one. When that happens, entertain the kids with the classic ABC game to enhance their observation skills and bring out their competitive natures. Before beginning this interactive game, set the rules to avoid any sibling squabbles. For instance, you can establish that each child must find their assigned letter within a word on a license plate, billboard, or street sign or they must find a full word that begins with their chosen letter. Start with the letter A and see which child can find the letter first. Keep tally of the points for each child who finds the letter first to total up after you finish with the letter Z. Or, form teams so the game is more cooperative. With twenty-six letters in the alphabet, this activity is sure to provide loads of entertainment in the car.

○ PLAY TWENTY QUESTIONS IN THE CAR

AGES 8-12

Get creative when running errands with a game of Twenty Questions. To play the game, designate one child as the leader and have this child silently find an object either in the car or along the road. Next, each child participating gets a chance to ask a yes or no question to find clues before guessing. The primary rule is that no more than twenty questions can be asked. If one of the children guesses the object before twenty questions are asked, he or she wins. If no one can guess the object, then the leader wins that round. Repeat the process until you reach your destination to keep the kids focused on the game versus the length of the trip.

○ HOST A ROAD TRIP PAPER CLIP GAME

AGES 6-12

Turn a simple object like a paper clip into the foundation for a hilarious car game. This game prompts your kids to listen intently to what others have to say. The object of the game is to have all children agree on one word that is forbidden. The game works best if you choose a common word such as *good* or *fun* or even something used all the time, such as *and*. Arm each child with a paper clip and head out on your road trip adventure. As the family is chatting, have your children listen closely for the forbidden word. If someone says the forbidden word, he or she loses the paper clip. The last child holding a paper clip wins that round. Start the game over with a different word and see just how long your children can make this activity last.

○ SPEAK IN PIG LATIN

Make learning a "new" language a fun part of your errand. Whether you are running to the dry cleaners or waiting in a line at the post office, this activity is bound to spark a few giggles. Pig Latin requires each person to leave out the first letter of a word and tack it on to the end of the word while adding an *ay* sound. For example, in order to say the phrase "Let's go play," your kids would say "Ets-lay o-gay lay-pay." Start this activity by saying a phrase in Pig Latin to see if they can identify what you are trying to say and then challenge each child to come up with their own phrase using this pseudo language. Not only does this activity teach your children how to practice sounds and learn about compound words, it also provides them with enter-tainment when they are bored while out and about.

○ SING WHAT YOU SAY

If you want to add a bit of fun to an ordinary day, challenge your children to sing what they say. Ideal for any age, you can launch this activity just about anywhere. Set the rules of the game by letting them know that they have to sing everything they want to say. For some healthy competition, start each child with a score of ten or twenty and deduct a point when one says something instead of sing-ing it. Challenge your older children to sing their phrases to a familiar tune and add a bit of variety to the activity by having another player continue the same tune while answering questions in a sing-song voice.

○ MAKE LICENSE PLATE LETTER PHRASES

Prompt your kids to look out the window versus sulk in the back seat when playing this game while taking a car ride. While there are many variations to the license plate game, this activity helps test your kids' abilities to form words and phrases. Set the guidelines for the activity by stipulating that each child must choose a license plate and come up with a phrase based on the letters available. For example, if the license plate reads "DPWF," the player must make a phrase using the letters, such as "Don't play with frogs." You can have all players come up with different phrases for one license plate or allow each child to choose his or her own license plate to decipher. Mom and Dad can join in and showcase their skills as wordsmiths too.

○ PLAY GUESS WHO?

Let all the family secrets surface when playing a game of Guess Who? With just a tad bit of knowledge about their siblings or parents, your kids can help reveal what they know about their family members. With this game, each child secretly chooses a member of the family to "dish" on, without revealing who holds the secret. For example, your oldest child may say "Guess who snores when he or she sleeps?" and then the rest of the group must guess who is guilty. The first person to guess correctly wins that round. Move to the next child in the group who can share a secret about another family member or even the same sibling or parent. If your kids can't think of secrets, consider having everyone write something about themselves on a piece of paper, throw the paper in a hat or bowl, and pick out one to read aloud and have everyone guess.

○ TALLY UP STATE STATISTICS

Make local travel much more interesting by playing a game that helps teach your children more about geography. While traveling in the US, prompt your children to spot a license plate from each state to occupy their time. For younger children, it may be helpful to supply them with a list of the fifty states in the US. To occupy older children, ask them to make a list of the states prior to playing the game. Then, while driving along, have your kids check off the state from their list when they see a license plate on a car from that state driving by. If your children thrive on competition, consider awarding points to the first player to find each state and tally up the results once license plates from all fifty states have been found.

○ PLAY THE BIG GAME

Even your little ones will enjoy using their imagination in big ways when playing the Big Game. This game prompts kids to dig deep into their creative minds for a bigger answer. The object of the game is to start by naming a small object such as a paper clip, a push pin, or even a pea. Then, the next player in the group must name an object slightly larger, such as a cherry tomato or a small bouncy ball. As each child takes a turn, he or she must keep the game going by naming an object that is larger than the previous object named. If a player cannot name an object, he or she is skipped until the next turn. Once the game comes to a stall, the last person to name an object is deemed the winner.

○ DECORATE A ROAD TRIP PILLOWCASE

If you're heading out for a longer car ride, this activity might help get your kids excited for the trip. Before you get started, purchase a white pillowcase for each child or bleach existing pillowcases so your children have a blank slate. Then, while lining out each pillowcase on a table or the floor of your garage, arm the kids with fabric markers, fabric paints, and paintbrushes. The fun begins when they start bringing the pillowcases to life with drawings or special phrases. If you are about to head out on a road trip or family vacation, encourage the kids to make illustrations related to the area you plan to visit so they have a souvenir they can use on the trip and well after you return home.

○ BALANCE BOOKS AT THE LIBRARY

If the thrill of reading adventures wears off the next time you're at the library, test their balancing acts with this activity. In a quiet area of the library, ask each child to choose a paperback book and line up along the wall. Next, have each participant place the paperback book on top of their heads. See how long each child can stand with the book in place. Then, ramp up the challenge by asking the group to balance books while standing on one leg or while walking a few feet down an aisle of the library. You can even time the children to see how long they can balance with one or two paperback books placed on top of their noggins.

○ PLAY NAME THAT TREE ON A HIKE

Trekking through the woods is an adventure in itself, but if your children are getting tired or cranky before you have made it to your destination, provide them with a challenge that helps them look a little more closely at the nature surrounding them. Give your older children a chance to help educate younger siblings by launching a game of Name That Tree. Although many trees look similar and are often described as "tall" or "green," your children may just surprise you with their knowledge of the forest while on a family hike. The object of the game is to correctly name the type of tree that stands before you. Whether it is a yellow birch, evergreen, maple, oak, or pine tree, ask your kids to wager a guess and award points to the first child to correctly name that tree. Younger kids who don't know the names might enjoy pointing out the differences among the trees—leaf shape, bark style, height, etc.

○ MAKE A TRAIL MAP ON A HIKE

Teach your children about navigation with this screen-free activity designed for when you are exploring nature at a nearby park or on a hiking trail while on vacation. Armed with notebooks and pens, set out on the hiking trail and encourage the kids to take note of land-marks they see, such as colorful trees, rock formations, and streams. Ask them to make notations in their notebook by stopping at various points of the hike and writing down a clear landmark that could help guide them back to the beginning of the trail. Once you reach the top of the mountain or a good stopping point of the trail, turn around and head back to where you started, letting the kids lead the way while following their trail maps.

○ COLLECT PINECONES

Taking a walk can turn into an adventure when you send your kids on a hunt for pinecones. With a bag or basket in tow, you can host pinecone races or make creative crafts once the collection is complete. Whether you are venturing through the neighborhood park or walking through the forest, pinecones are typically easy to find. Form your kids into teams to collect these remnants of pine trees to make the day even more interesting. Host a race to see who can find the most in the least amount of time when carrying a stopwatch with you on your walk. Once the bags or baskets are full, brainstorm ideas with your children to determine how to display their assortment of pinecones. For example, you can paint the pinecones to display in your home or tie ribbon around them to make door decor. Whatever they choose to create, they can feel good about finding the treasures all on their own.

○ SEARCH FOR SEASHELLS

You don't have to be a beach expert to find the most unique seashells along the shore. In fact, your kids can entertain themselves looking for the most interesting or brightly colored seashells with just a few tips. Whether you're vacationing on the beach or just taking a day trip to one, your kids will love bringing home a seashell souvenir. Start by heading to the shoreline to find seashells before walking a few feet into the water to find seashells in shallow water. Make sure nonswimmers are equipped with flotation devices or life jackets. You can also find seashells in rocky areas or parts of the beach covered in seaweed. Have your troop bring their bags of seashells back to your lounging area to compare shapes and sizes.

○ BUILD A SAND CASTLE

AGES 6–12

After a day splashing around in the water, keep your kids from getting bored by building a sand castle. From a small construction to an elaborate castle with levels and layers, tap into your kids' creative skills by challenging them to build without limits. One of the easiest ways to get started is to begin packing moist sand into a plastic bucket. Add a bit of water to the bucket to get a firm shape before flipping the bucket over for the first level of your sand castle. Repeat the process and line up the towers of sand in a row. Use different-sized buckets to create a towering effect. Older children can add some detail by drawing designs in the sand with a stick or even creating a small lake or river that flows in front of the castle for added effect.

○ MAKE SNOW ANGELS ON A SKI TRIP

AGES 6–12

Although a ski trip with your kids is a thrilling adventure in itself, there may be times when your children need to be entertained while waiting in line for the lift or once they have reached the bottom of the slope. Bring out their inner angels with this activity during your downtime. Show your children how to make outlines in the snow beyond creating a snowman. Have each child pick an area filled with snow but off the beaten path, preferably on flat ground. Then, each child should lay down flat on the ground, firmly packing their bodies into the snow. Instruct them to place their arms out to the sides and then move them toward the head and then back to their sides to create the angel wings. The same motions should be made with their legs to create the base of the angel. If you have a group of children, have each one create snow angels in a line. The only thing left to do is get up and admire the angel outlines.

LOOK FOR ANIMAL TRACKS IN THE SNOW

AGES 8-12

Whether you're on a fun snow-filled vacation or just trekking through town, take the chill off with a scavenger hunt. Help your children identify critter tracks based on which animals live in your geographic area. Have each child try to guess the type of animal making the imprints in the fluffy white snow and discuss how these animals survive in frigid environments. Not only do your children get to engage in a hunt for animals, but they may also learn a few things about critters and their habitats along the way.

HOST TUG-OF-WAR AT THE PARK

AGES 8-12

If siblings are squabbling while taking turns on the swings and jungle gym at the park, transform the tension into a healthy competition with a game of tug-of-war. All you need is a long piece of rope or a jump rope to tug around with this activity. This activity works best when you have four or more children with you. Form teams for the competition and put an even amount of children on each side. Tie a ribbon or scarf to the center of the rope and place a stick on the ground toward the end of each side of the rope. Once the kiddos start tugging on each side, the team that tugs the ribbon or scarf to the stick on the opposite side wins. Make sure that your children are wearing tennis shoes for this activity to avoid any injuries when the tugging gets vigorous. If you have gloves lying around, kids might want to put them on to avoid rope burn.

○ PLAY STICK WARS

Put a twist on your next family nature walk with a Stick Wars game. No, it's not a swordfight—it's actually a contest to see who can find the biggest stick along the trail to use as a walking stick, then decorate at home. As you're walking along discussing the types of trees and flowers you see on the path, ask each child to be on the lookout for sticks lying loose on the ground. Make sure they know that thick branches are off limits for this game. To start the competition, appoint one child to choose a stick from the path. Designate how much farther the group must walk before the next player attempts to choose a bigger stick. Continue the process until each child has had a chance to pick up a stick. Then, line up all children and have them compare the lengths of their sticks to declare a winner. Take the sticks home to decorate with yarn, glitter glue, or even acrylic paint so they can display them like trophies.

○ COUNT THE SEMIS ON THE ROAD

AGES 8–12

Make a simple road trip much more interesting and educational with this counting game. As you're cruising down the highway, occupy the kids in a way that tests their ability to count well into the double digits. Challenge each player to count the number of semis or tractor trailer trucks they see on the road. You can have each child count to themselves or play this activity with a group, working collaboratively to reach a certain number. If you want to add some competition to the activity, set a timer and give each child a portion of time to spot the semis. The child who finds the most semis within the time limit or within a designated distance wins.

○ BUILD A BIRD'S NEST

Keep your little ones crafty and quiet while playing at the park or lounging around at a campsite when on vacation with an activity that teaches them more about nature. You don't need live birds to imagine a flock resting in your kids' homemade birds' nest. Before sending your kids out to find materials, discuss how birds create nests for their babies. Make sure your children can visualize a bird's nest and then see if they can find small sticks and leaves to construct their own. Small sticks may need to be intertwined carefully by older children while the younger children place leaves in the center of the makeshift nest. If you want to use the nest as a decoration for your home, help older children spray-paint the exterior once you get home so you can display their work.

○ PLAY GROCERY MEMORY MATH

Whether you need several bags of groceries or just a few, make the trip much more enjoyable by prompting your children to test their memories and their math skills. Grocery memory math is ideal for tweens who can do some rounding and mental math. All you need to do is shop while your children carefully observe the items you toss into the cart. Let each one see the items and the prices. They should keep a running tally of your total bill by rounding the prices (for example, rounding $2.99 to $3). Once you reach the checkout lane, have each child estimate the total cost of the groceries before tax is applied. The player closest to the price without going over the total wins. Be sure to restrict calculators from this game.

○ PLAY WOULD YOU RATHER? IN LINE AT THE STORE

AGES 8–12

See just how witty your children can be when standing in long lines at the store with a game of Would You Rather? While long store lines commonly bring out the whines, this game will make your children look forward to waiting. The game Would You Rather? prompts your children to think about choices they would make. Often comical, the questions may include "Would you rather eat a bug or step on a spider?" or "Would you rather clean the bathtub or clean your brother's room?" Choose one child to start asking questions and a child to answer honestly. You can also have one child pose questions while the remaining children all answer the questions.

○ CREATE ZOO SKETCHES

AGES 6–12

When you're heading out for a day at the zoo, have your kids create a souvenir of their adventurous day when toting along paper, pencils, and sketchbooks. Ideal for day trips to the zoo or when you are chaperoning your child's field trip, this activity prompts your little ones to capture every single detail of the animal excursion. While it may seem more convenient to ask your children to draw sketches of the animals while you are on your way home, the point of this activity is to help them use their observational skills immediately. Line up the children on a bench or a row of chairs once you find the perfect exhibit of birds, monkeys, or zebras, and hand each child a sketchbook or piece of paper. Using pens, pencils, or colored pencils, have each member of the zoo troop begin drawing the animal or animals directly in front of them. With an immediate visual, they can capture even the smallest details of the animals to later showcase to family members and friends.

○ CONNECT THE DOTS

AGES 6-12

A long ride in a car, train, or plane often leaves kids feeling restless. When boredom sets in, show them how just a few dots can keep them entertained. Pack a few pieces of 8½" x 11" white paper and pens for the trip and ask each child to create ten rows of ten dots. The end result forms a square of dots on the page. Next, challenge each child to create a drawing on the page by connecting the dots. For instance, the pen must travel from one dot to another to form a triangle or an octagon. See who can be the most creative and form a shape or illustration by connecting the dots. Have mom and dad judge the drawings before launching another round of connect the dots.

○ TEST YOUR CHOPSTICK SKILLS

AGES 8-12

Provide the kids with some entertainment when eating at a restaurant that offers chopsticks as utensils. While learning how to use chopsticks to pick up food is fun in and of itself, challenge your children to do more with this fun activity. Begin by placing objects from your purse or bag on the table and have each child take turns trying to pick it up with the chopsticks. For example, you may have a clean tissue handy they can try to pick up or even a tube of lipstick. Make the game much more interesting by having your children choose objects already on the table, such as utensils or napkins, to manipulate with the chopsticks. You can award points for each item successfully picked up with the chopsticks and tally the scores once the meal arrives.

○ MAKE UP WEIRD WORDS

While your children may be familiar with I Spy, you can help them to spy objects while also developing their language skills. Making up weird words requires some imagination, yet no doubt will result in fits of laughter while on the road or while keeping the kids entertained on a shopping trip. The goal of this activity is to transform real words into weird words by substituting the first letter of a word with another letter. For example, if you are at the grocery store and one child spots a tub of butter, he can say, "I spy lutter" instead of "butter." The leader of the game cannot name a real word when substituting out the first letter of the object. With butter, real words like mutter and putter are not allowed. Once the weird word is announced, each child then has to try to guess the object.

○ CREATE A BUBBLES CONTEST AT THE PARK

Make a routine day at the park a bubbly adventure for the bubbly personalities in your crew. Armed with just a few bottles of bubbles and blowing sticks, you can transform a visit to the park into a bubble wonderland. Before heading out for a day at the playground, fill up your daily bag with a few bottles of bubbles. If you have large bubble wands lying around, toss those in, too, to entertain the kids when the thrill of the slides and jungle gym has lost its effect. Break out the bottles of bubbles and challenge your kids to see who can blow the largest bubble of the group. Little ones can also try to hold the bubbles on their fingertips until they pop. See who can keep their bubbles afloat the longest to add an element of healthy competition to this activity.

◯ PLAY SHOPPING LINE CHARADES

AGES 6–10

Beat boredom while waiting in line at a department or grocery store with a good old game of charades. Theme this game to fit the store for a little more fun. While standing next to your shopping cart, gather your children around and launch a game of charades to keep them occupied. Choose one child to pick a word or phrase to act out while the other children must take turns wagering a guess. Limit the words or phrases to items in your cart or items along the checkout aisle to simplify the game for younger children. For example, if you're in a clothing store, have them act out the word *shirt* or *pants*. If you're shopping at the grocery store, have them choose a food item in plain view. Once the word or phrase is guessed by another, take turns to let another child shine in the spotlight as the actor.

◯ PACK A TOY PICNIC

AGES 6–10

Excite your kids with a new kind of picnic plan for the day. After a filling lunch, pack up a picnic basket with fun toys and games and head off to the park for some fresh air and a new scenic area to explore those toys they may have forgotten even existed. Make this activity a group effort by asking each child to secretly choose one or two toys to pack into the basket. Once you get to the park, allow the children to pick out one toy at a time, describing what he or she brought so the others can guess. Then play with the toy as a group and move on to the next toy. You may even find that your little ones are more apt to share when they can present the toy to the others.

○ CREATE SUGAR PACKET SHAPES

When dining out, children are prone to getting impatient, especially when hungry or tired. Pass the time with items on your table by challenging them to make sugar packet shapes. Gather a few sweetener or sugar packets from the table and ask each child to make a shape with a few of the packets. (Make sure they carefully handle each one so as not to break the package.) Each child can test her imagination. For instance, one child may choose to build a tower while another may create a heart on the table using the packets. Take this activity to another level by incorporating packages of crackers into the designs. Once the food arrives, have the group clean up the packets so they are readily available for use by the next set of diners.

○ MAKE SAND PICTURES

While there are plenty of activities to keep your kids busy at the beach, when you have some downtime or the kids are tired of splashing in the water, try making sand pictures they can admire until the next wave washes away their designs. Begin by asking your children to find objects they can use to draw shapes or words in the sand, such as a stick, the handle of a beach shovel, or the end of an umbrella. Next, give each child a portion of the sand to create a message or snazzy design. One child may want to draw out his name in the sand while another may want to draw a stick figure. Encourage your kids to share their tools and interchange objects for thicker or thinner lines in the sand. The only thing left to do is stand back and admire the artwork.

○ START A GOOD DAY/BAD DAY DISCUSSION

Sometimes, a healthy discussion can occupy the time and keep your children entertained for a while. Encourage them to speak up and share their thoughts and feelings with a Good Day/Bad Day activity. The object of this activity is to have each member of your family share what was good about his or her day and what was bad about his or her day. Ideal for rides in the car, this game prompts your children to share their activities while also learning more about each sibling or friend along for the ride. Begin by sharing something positive that you remember about your day, such as waking up to the bright sun. Then, have each person share the good. Although it may sound dreary to have your kids share bad things about the day, you get a chance to point out the positive that evolved as a result of the experience. For instance, if your child says she fell while riding her bike, you can point out that she was able to ride her bike a long distance, which is a significant accomplishment.

○ FINGER PAINT WITH FOOD

Make dessert time in a restaurant a bit more entertaining with a finger-painting activity. Make sure you have napkins nearby so you don't leave any messes behind for the waiter or waitress. As dessert is served, ask the server for some whipped cream on a separate plate. As your children are devouring their pie, cake, or ice cream, have them dip their finger into the whipped cream and add a bit to their dessert plate. Using a toothpick or even their fingers, have them swirl the whipped cream into shapes. See who can make the most creative design or even write their names on the plate using only the whipped cream. Although it is often frowned upon to play with your food, this activity is the exception, especially when your kids are looking for an entertaining end to their meal at a restaurant.

○ MAKE HOMEMADE TRAIL MIX FOR THE ROAD

AGES 6–12

■☐☐

Prepare a healthy and tasty snack for your next trip with some help from your little chefs. Find something to include in your homemade trail mix that appeals to everyone along for the travel as a surprise for when hunger strikes in the back seat. Begin by giving each child a small ziptop bag. Then, scour through the pantry for food items that would help make the trail mix both sweet and salty. For example, your kids can include small pretzels, nuts, crackers, bits of dried fruit, and a few small pieces of chocolate candy. Dry cereal also helps to add some fiber to your mix. Once you have all the ingredients lined up on the counter, form an assembly line and have each child add a handful of the food items to his or her sandwich bag. Fill enough bags for each member of the family to disperse during the trip.

○ TELL WEIRD STORIES

AGES 6–12

■☐☐

Storytelling is a favorite pastime for kids of all ages, and it comes in handy when you are traveling or waiting in line at the store. With this activity, your kids can get creative and weird when telling stories in a hurry. Set a timer or look at the time on your watch so you can stop the story after two minutes. Start by giving each child three words that must be included in the story, such as "birthday," "gorilla," and "airplane." Then, designate a child to tell his or her story first. Once the two minutes are up and the laughter has stopped, appoint another child to tell a two-minute story with three new odd words that must be included.

○ PLAY THE WHERE? GAME

■□□

If you have little ones who are always asking "why?" this game is the perfect solution when your kids are getting restless at the park, library, or in the car. The Where? game allows you to ask questions and prompt your kids to think critically. Start with something simple, such as "Where do we eat our dinner?" Appoint only one child to answer the question or have each child shout out the answer quickly. Next, pose more questions that begin with the word *where*, such as "Where do we like to go on Saturdays?" or "Where does Grandma live?" Try to stump them with questions about yourself, such as "Where does Mommy like to go with her friends?" or "Where does Daddy work?" While younger children may need a little help with general questions, you can challenge the older children by asking questions about their siblings' interests or their curriculum at school.

○ ORGANIZE HOTEL ROOM PICKUP

■□□

When it's time to check out of the hotel, prompt your kids to help clean up with a fun game that caters to their competitive natures. You don't even need to have the suitcases ready if you have just a few plastic bags. Pass out the plastic bags and assign each child a task that helps all of them fill up their bags. For example, one child has to fill up his bag with trash, such as empty cups, napkins, candy wrappers, or soda cans. Another child can be responsible for filling his bag with dirty clothes, which prompts him to check under the beds and in the corners of the room for socks. Additional bags can be filled with small toys or stuffed animals that were brought on vacation or even purchased as souvenirs. Make the game a race and see who can fill his or her bag first to get the kids moving quickly before you make the journey home.

○ TAKE A STICKY WALK

Turn your daily walk to the park or hike through the local trails into a sticky adventure with this activity. With a few strips of adhesive paper and a little creativity, your kids can get sticky without getting messy while exploring the great outdoors. For this activity, you'll need to create bracelets or anklets before starting the sticky journey. Using strips of fabric, measure each child's arm and ankle and then tie the fabric together so it creates a bracelet or anklet that won't slip off. Attach adhesive-backed paper (available at craft stores) to the outside of the fabric so the exterior is sticky. Then, while on your walk or hike, have the kids see what sticks to their bracelets and anklets. Items such as leaves, seeds, sand, or even dirt often collect on adhesive surfaces. Once you return from your excursion, see who has the most interesting items stuck to them.

○ ROAST PUMPKIN SEEDS

Make a trip to the pumpkin patch much more exciting with this activity. Start by selecting a few small pumpkins while at the store or while visiting a pumpkin patch. Then, help your kids carve the pumpkins to reveal the gooey inside full of pumpkin seeds. Rinse the seeds and let them dry on paper towels. Have the kids help you mix up a few tablespoons of vegetable oil and a teaspoon of salt in a bowl. Toss in the seeds and then put them on a cookie sheet. Bake them at 250°F for about an hour and once the seeds cool, let the kids enjoy the treat.

○ PLAY HOLIDAY WORD SCRAMBLE

Turn those holiday trips into an educational endeavor with this activity. Using a few words related to the closest holiday and a few handy notebooks and pens, you can help your kids form words and get into the holiday spirit while traveling. Begin by making a list of words related to the nearest holiday. For example, when it's close to Halloween, add words to the list such as *spooky*, *ghost*, or *witch*. Then, have the kids try to make words from the letters within each of these words. For instance, for the word *ghost*, your children may come up with words such as *hot* or *got*. See how many words your children can create before moving onto the next word while driving along the road. If you have competitive siblings, consider deeming the person with the most words the winner for that round.

○ INITIATE TOY ROTATION

If you're getting ready to take a road trip or traveling adventure, it's likely you have packed a few activity bags or allowed the kids to take along a few toys. However, those toys only entertain for just a short while. With this activity, let the fun last and show your kids how to share. The object of this activity is to let each child showcase her toys for the ride and then share them with siblings or friends riding along. From coloring books and crayons to stuffed animals or dolls, every toy gets plenty of use and your kids get to vary their entertainment for a short time. Begin by explaining that each child gets ten minutes to play with his toy and then once the time is up, the toy must rotate to the next child. When you have three or more children in the car, this activity can last awhile and keep those little minds entertained.

○ PLAY WASHABLE WORD GUESS

AGES 8–12

When lounging at the community pool with your kids, the last thing you want to hear is "I'm bored," but it happens. A washable word guess game only requires a group of kids willing to get creative. Line up the kids in a row and have the child at the end of the line trace one word lightly with a finger on the back of the child directly in front of him or her. That child must then guess the word. If the guess is correct, the writer is out of the game and the child who guessed correctly gets to write the next word. When a child guesses incorrectly, he is out and must move from the line. You can also host this game similar to a game of telephone and have each child trace the same word, but what they may find is that the word is not the same once the last child has traced it.

○ HOST A FUNNY FACE CHALLENGE

AGES 6–12

It usually doesn't take much to make little kids laugh, but if your older kids are sullen when riding along in the car, host a funny face challenge to turn those frowns upside down. Using a handheld mirror from a compact, have one child hold the mirror while another child tells him what type of emotion to express. For example, if the child says "happy," then the kid holding the mirror must smile. If the child says "confused," then the child holding the mirror must contort her face to show this emotion or expression. Have older kids get creative by seeing how unique they can get with the commands, such as "sleepy" or "winking." If the person holding the mirror doesn't crack a smile, it's likely the rest of the crew will not be able to keep a straight face.

○ START A SPEED-TALKING CHALLENGE

AGES 6–12
■ ■ □

Indulge the little chatterboxes in your crew with a game that lets them chatter away while taking a walk or riding in the car. Ideal for long trips or even short breaks while out and about, this activity keeps your kids talking and laughing at the same time. The object of the game is to see who can talk the fastest. Choose a well-known poem or fairy tale for this activity that everyone in your group knows well. For example, you can have each child recite the ABCs or even "Twinkle, Twinkle, Little Star." Start by appointing the first player and then with a stop watch, time how long it takes for him or her to recite the poem or assigned phrase. Then, give each child a chance to beat the score. The player who recites the phrase or poem the fastest wins.

○ MAKE A GROCERY STORE PICTURE BOOK

AGES 6–12
■ ■ □

Turn preparation for a trip to the grocery store into an art extravaganza with this project. Instead of making a boring old list of items you need, let the kids help by illustrating your grocery list. Give each child a few index cards or small pieces of paper and jot down a few items you need from the store, such as milk, potatoes, or bread. Then, let the kids draw the items with a pencil. Have them color in the item with crayons or markers, and then gather all pieces of paper or index cards and make your way to the store. While you are shopping, have your kids sift through the colorful items and identify what you need from the cards or illustrations on paper. Make this activity even more fun by shuffling the cards and distributing them to your children. As you find each item, the child holding the card (or illustrated piece of paper) gets a point.

◯ PLAY STUFFED-ANIMAL HIDE-AND-SEEK

Just because you're traveling doesn't mean your kids can't enjoy a game of hide-and-seek. With just a few stuffed animals brought from home, you can launch this activity while at a family member's home or even in a hotel room. Have each child offer one of his toys or stuffed animals as the object to hide. Then, choose one player and one item and send him or her off to hide the object while the other kids have their eyes closed. Then, let the hunt begin. When in hotel rooms, remind your kids to search under the beds, in drawers, and even in the bathtub. You can also alter this activity and have each child hide an object at the same time and see which player is able to find the most treasures.

◯ PLAY ROAD TRIP RHYMING

If you have some budding poets in your crew, this activity is bound to keep them from getting bored while on a road trip, regardless if you are traveling in a car, train, or airplane. With just a moment of brainstorming for words, your kids can bust out some rhymes to keep themselves entertained. Start by jotting down a few words on a sheet of paper, such as car, fish, book, or pen. For younger kids, stick with one-syllable words to simplify the activity while you can use more advanced two-syllable words with older children. The object of the game is to have your children think of as many words as possible that rhyme with a word on the list. They can say them aloud or make a list if you prefer to have a few moments of silence. The child with the most words that rhyme wins that round. Then, you're ready to start the next round with the next word on the list.

○ CREATE SECRET HANDSHAKES

When you're out and about and your kids' hands are fidgety, this activity is ideal. Pair up your children, or if you're with an only child while on a road trip, join in on the fun. Have the pair create a secret handshake. The handshake may consist of clapping their hands together, fist bumping, bashing their forearms together, or a combination of all three. They can even add dance moves or a hip shake to the choreography. Not only will their secret handshake allow them to communicate with each other, but it also gives them something to giggle about when showcasing the routine for Mom and Dad.

○ PLAY THE TELEPHONE GAME

Make a trip to the zoo, an amusement park, or a local museum much more enjoyable, especially while waiting in line, by playing the telephone game. This age-old game tests your kids' listening skills and may even produce a comical result. Begin by explaining the object of the game. One person starts by whispering a phrase into another person's ear. The phrase should be about five to eight words and can be something funny or simple, such as "The cat jumped over the moon." Then, that person passes the message on to the next child. The key to the game is to whisper the phrase so no one else can hear it. Then, once the message reaches the last child in line, have him or her say the phrase. What your children just might find is that if they don't listen carefully, they could end up with a phrase that is drastically different by the time it filters through each player.

○ MAKE RESTAURANT STRAW ART

■□□

It can be grueling to wait for your food to be delivered when the kids are antsy. Keep them entertained with a fun activity using the straws on your table. Unwrap the straws on your table and instead of using them for your beverages, help your kids make straw art. Kids can bend them into shapes, tie them together, or line them up on the table to create a flat work of art. Encourage your children to work together to build one giant tower or sculpture by intertwining the straws, too. If the restaurant server is willing to spare a few more straws, you can make straw art with your kids and use a straw to sip out those milkshakes or cold beverages while waiting for your food.

○ HOST A THUMB WRESTLING COMPETITION

■■□

When your kids need something athletic to do but you don't have a field or ball available, try this activity. While on a road trip or while taking a break at the park, launch a game of thumb wrestling to test your kids' hand-eye coordination. Pair your children with a partner or sibling who has similar athletic abilities. Make sure you set the rules before the wrestling match begins, explaining that the children must keep their wrists positioned on the table and cannot use their other hand to assist with a win. To thumb wrestle, have two players touch their thumbs together and lock their fingers together while their wrists are situated firmly on a table. Then, let the thumb wiggling (or wrestling) begin. The first child to secure the other player's thumb wins that round. When playing with partners, you can also host a tournament, pairing the winners of each round together to deem an overall champion.

◯ MAKE UP TONGUE TWISTERS

If you have little chatterboxes in your crew, launch this activity while traveling or waiting in line at the grocery store. Ideal for both young and older children, this activity is designed to keep them talking while twisting up their tongues. Start by asking each child to repeat a common tongue twister, such as "Sally sells seashells by the sea-shore." Let each participant try to recite the tongue twister slowly first and then as fast as possible, over and over again. Once they have mastered the tongue twister, challenge your kids to make up their own. Explain that each starting letter of the words in the phrase must be the same. You can even assign a letter to each child and offer a few suggestions for words. Then, let them try to recite the phrases without twisting up their tongues (and while holding in laughter).

◯ PREDICT TRAVEL TIMES

If cries of "Are we there yet?" are coming from the back seat during a road trip, let your kids answer themselves! All you need is a paper map your kids can open up, view, and analyze to get this activity going. Point out your starting location on the map and then circle the destination. Ask each child to trace the route with his or her finger and then guess how long it will take to get from point A to point B. While older kids may want to use their math skills to calculate the time based on the map scale, your younger children may just want to venture a guess. Let each child know what time it is and have them tell you what time they think you will arrive. Write down all responses and cross off those guesses once the time has passed. The child who guesses closest to your arrival time wins the game.

◯ PLAY WHAT HAPPENED ON THIS DAY?

AGES 8-12
■■■

If you're taking a trip to the library and one of your kids needs more time, let the others try this activity. The What Happened on This Day? game is ideal for inquisitive minds that want to learn about historical events. Start by asking the librarian where you can find archives of newspapers. With an adult's help, the kids can access microfiche files or look through old stacks of newspapers bound in a book at the library. Start by looking up newspaper dates to find the same day as the day of your trip, but on a different year. You can read the headlines to your younger children and discuss the events of the day. Your older children can dig a little deeper and search through newspaper archives to find the day they were born to read more about what happened on the day of their births.

◯ FIND THE ROUTE NUMBER

AGES 6-12
■■☐

Keep the kids entertained and observant while on a road trip with this scavenger hunt to find route numbers on the highway. Before heading out for a highway adventure, help the kids scour through maps to determine the route numbers you may see along the way. While in your vehicle, arm each child with a notepad and pencil to write down the route numbers they see on the signs. The child who finds all the route numbers first wins that round. You can even alter this activity to include exit numbers or even names of cities while on the road.

○ PLAY "IF I LIVED HERE..."

While taking in the scenery on a long drive may occupy your children for a short while, this activity keeps them busy and entertained for a bit longer. Encourage your kids to imagine what it would be like to live in another area. As you are trudging along on a road trip, ask each child to guess what it would be like to live in the cities you pass along the way. Have each child start the sentence with "If I lived here..." and then allow them to finish the sentence with activities they would engage in or have them point out a home along the route they would like to live in. Discuss the attractions in the area and let your children detail the type of friends they would meet or the jobs they would take as adults if they lived in each city you pass.

○ LAUNCH A MEMORY GAME ON VACATION

If regular memory games are getting old, try this new twist to the memory game. While standing in line at an amusement park or driving along the road, start the game by quizzing your children about recent events. Questions such as "What did we eat for dinner on Tuesday night?" or "Who was your first-grade teacher?" are easier to navigate for younger children. Put your older children to the test with questions such as "What is Mom's middle name?" or "How old were you when you started walking?" Keep tally of how many questions your children get right to add a competitive component to the activity. You can also prompt your kids to come up with questions to test each other's memories.

◯ CREATE CAR AMUSEMENT CENTERS

If your kids are easily bored on car rides, create an amusement center in the back seat that will leave them wanting to run errands with you. With a fabric shoe rack or bag with pockets you can easily tie to the back of the front seats, you can have the kids help you create an activity center filled with their favorite toys and games. Start by asking your children to select a few small toys from their rooms before heading to the car. For example, you can place a doll or small plastic fire engine in one of the pockets and a coloring book and crayons in another pocket. Add a few granola bars, snacks, and bottles of water to quench their hunger and thirst, as well as a few small games and puzzles to keep them entertained. Before each road trip, swap out the toys for new activities, such as word find books and even comic books so your kids are surprised to find new things to play with on the road.

◯ EXPLORE "IF I WERE A..."

Get your kids to think creatively and critically when launching a game of "If I were a…" when you're out and about. This activity lets you see just how wild your kids' imaginations are when they are trying to entertain others in your crew. Set the tone by offering your own example to start. You can begin by saying, "If I were a monkey, I would swing from trees and wave to people on the streets." Or, you can focus on a kid-friendly celebrity, such as "If I were Elmo, I would sing a funny song to make people laugh." Then, select one child to share her sentence. Make sure each kid explains why she chose the person or animal, and details her rationale for the actions. Ask why your child wants to swing from trees or sing funny songs to help her think about her choices.

○ TALK TO FLOWERS

Even if your kids are a bit shy, this activity is bound to get them talking while you are visiting a flower garden or botanical museum. The act of talking to flowers may seem a little strange at first, but they'll likely get into it after a few minutes. While walking through a flower garden at your local botanical center, horticulture center, or even a lawn and garden store, talk with your children about how plants and flowers benefit from loving care just like people do. While it may seem a little silly, you can keep them entertained and comfortable helping create blooming buds by starting the conversation. A phrase such as "How are you today?" is often a good start. You can also have the kids pick one plant or flower and have them talk about themselves.

○ PLAY MARCO POLO AT THE POOL

A day at the pool is bound to produce some laughter and fun, but when the kids get bored, launch this activity to keep them engaged and working together. Marco Polo is an age-old game that might be new to your children. The object of the game is to designate one child as "Marco" while in the pool. With his eyes closed, he must say Marco while the rest of the children randomly say "Polo." Keeping his eyes closed, he must detect where the other children are in the pool and tag them. This game gets interesting when your children are swimming about in the pool to get away from "Marco." Make sure the rules are clear that you must stay in a certain section of the pool while playing the game so "Marco" has a fair chance to tag each child.

○ WALK AND TOSS

Test your kids' coordination and balance when taking a hike or a morning jaunt through the park. All you need are a few pebbles or rocks and a little energy to walk and toss. Start by having your children choose a small rock or pebble and then line up each child to begin the game. Have the first player gently toss his rock on the path. The next player should try to toss his rock as close as possible to the first player's rock on the path. Continue letting each child toss his rock to see whose rock is closest to the first rock thrown. Once the winner is determined, have each child walk to the place where the winning rock was thrown and start the game all over again, moving forward. You can also alternate who gets to throw the rock first.

○ FLY KITES IN THE PARK

Instead of lamenting a windy day, grab a few kites and make the most of it. Start by distributing the kites to each child, showing younger children how to hold the kite's base. Then, demonstrate how to start walking or running through a grassy area while the wind picks up the top of the kite and sends it soaring. Then, space out your children in an open area and let them try it one at a time or together. Make sure you are far from trees to avoid any kites getting tangled or stuck in areas where you cannot reach. It may also help to partner children together so older kids can help the little ones manage the kite as it takes off into the air.

○ PLAY ROCK, PAPER, SCISSORS

Solve all sibling squabbles when out and about with a simple game of Rock, Paper, Scissors. From determining who gets to order first at a restaurant to which child gets to board a ride first at an amusement park, this fun game not only helps solve arguments, but it also gives your kids a fun way to interact with one another. The object of the game is to count to three and then have the players shape their hands into a rock, paper, or scissors. To make a rock, you form a fist, while paper represents just putting your hand out straight. To make scissors, you extend the first and middle fingers and separate them. The rules of the game stipulate that rock trumps scissors, paper covers rock, and scissors cut paper. Even if you don't have a dilemma to solve, this game can keep the kids busy while riding in the car or standing in line at the store.

○ CONNECT THE WORDS

Try this word game when you're waiting in line somewhere. To begin, start by explaining to the kids that when one person says a word, the next child must say a word that begins with the last letter of the previous word. Ideal for tweens, this game requires your children to know how to spell the words used. You can also modify the game for younger children by using simple words such as *cat* or *dog*. Once the first child chooses a word, such as *book*, then the next child must say a word that begins with *k*, such as *kind*. The next player must then say a word that begins with the letter *d*.

○ ADD UP INGREDIENTS

If your kids get restless and whiny while grocery shopping, get them involved in the process of choosing food for your daily meals. Perfect for the health-conscious family, this activity shows your children how to read product labels and compare products. Start by referencing your grocery list as you enter the store. Choose an item, such as crackers, and head to the snack aisle to begin comparing products. Ask each child to choose a different box of crackers and point out the calories, fat content, amount of sugar included in each serving, and the salt content. Discuss the differences among carbohydrates, fat, protein, and sugar, and how a healthy diet involves a balance of each. Older kids can even configure the amount of calories or fat in each serving doing simple math. Once the activity is complete, move on to the next product.

○ FIND FUNNY BOAT NAMES

A day at the beach or marina is often a treat for your kids, but if they're starting to run on empty, take a break with this quiet activity. When sitting on the shore or walking through the boat docks, test your kids' observation abilities. Have your kids walk by the boats at the marina and read the names of the boats to each other. Most boat owners proudly display the names of their boats, and while some are named after family members, others are quite comical. The object is to find the funniest boat name, such as In Sea-son or Reel Time. You can also alter this activity by asking the kids to find the largest or smallest boat and predict which boat can go the fastest on the water.

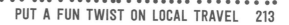

○ HUNT FOR THE CHEAPER ITEM

While many times when shopping your children bombard you with chants of "I want this," this activity can help show them the value of money and save you a few bucks at the same time. The object of the game is to find the cheapest item on your list. Before you begin shopping, show your crew how to find the price tags, whether they are located on clothing items or posted on signs in a grocery store. Then, announce the item you need and see who can find the item that is priced the lowest. While younger children may need some help reading the prices, you can give your older children a challenge and have them determine if buying in bulk saves you money. For example, if a set of twelve juice boxes is priced at $4.99 but a set of six juice boxes is $3.29, see if your kids can calculate how much you would be paying for each individual juice box.

○ TAKE CHARGE FOR FIFTEEN MINUTES

Parenting can be exhausting when you're the one making rules and enforcing them. Show your children how to take on some responsibility by letting them be the one in charge for a short time while out and about. Whether you are on the playground, taking a hike, or walking through the store, give your kids the opportunity to call the shots while you get to be a carefree kid. Start by explaining the rules of the activity. For fifteen minutes, one child gets to be the one in charge, which means he or she must tell the others what to do (Mom and Dad included) and has to find ways to enforce the rules. For example, your child could direct the group through the path on a hike, offering safety tips along the way, or she could help the little ones navigate the playground while keeping a close eye on all siblings. Rotate each child through fifteen minutes of being in charge and enjoy a little free time as a kid.

○ GUESS THE TEMPERATURE

A long drive offers scenic views for your children to admire, but if they're getting restless, launch a weather-inspired activity to keep them guessing and learning. The object of this game is to guess the temperature as you are driving through various areas. First, have a discussion about varying temperatures in the area where you are driving. Then, talk about highs and lows and how the temperature changes frequently, even within minutes. Next, have each child predict the temperature while you are inside the car. You can have them document this in a notebook or journal or have one sheet of paper for the combined guesses. The child who guesses the closest to the actual temperature wins that round. In order to determine the exact temperature without handheld electronics, turn on the weather station in the car, use your car's thermometer, or stop at a rest stop and ask the information center for verification.

○ MAKE A TOAST

You don't have to be an adult at a wedding to make a toast. In fact, you can keep kids entertained and show them a thoughtful way to express thanks by teaching them about toasts. First, explain the principles behind delivering a toast. Have your kids brainstorm a few things they would like to say and then let them take turns giving an impromptu speech. For example, your son could talk about how he is thankful for the food and the opportunity to be with his family while your daughter may want to toast a friend who is along for the meal or picnic. You can even prompt them to say funny things about each other or sing one another's praises during their toasts.

○ HOST A ROUND TABLE DISCUSSION

AGES 8-12

When dining out, it can be difficult to entertain the kids while you are waiting for beverages or food to be delivered to your table. Use this time to spark a round table discussion. Start with a general topic to get the conversation going. Things like your favorite food or the best thing that happened today are easy for younger kids. Get your kids involved with picking topics, too, by writing a few topics down on strips of a napkin and then drawing one out of a hat or bread basket to discuss. Your kids may choose to talk about sports, school, friends, or even family members. When the conversation goes dry, choose another topic or ask questions so your kids can think deeper about what they want to say.

○ LISTEN FOR SOUNDS OF SILENCE

AGES 6-12

Silence is often rare, especially when traveling with children. However, you can soak in the silence with this activity designed for families on the move. The object of the game is to help your kids observe their surroundings. Arm each child with a notebook, piece of paper, or small journal. Then, as you're riding along, ask them to close their eyes for one minute, soaking in the sounds while completely silent. Once the minute is up, have each child write down the sounds heard during their minute of solitude. If your children have duplicate answers, cross them out on the page. Then, tally up who has the most unique sounds to determine the winner of the game. You can play this game as many times as possible when traveling through new areas with the windows rolled down in the car.

○ PLAY THE HUMMING GAME

AGES 6–12

A sing-along is always fun when you are driving with the kids or taking a walk through the neighborhood. If you want to keep the music alive, yet at a lower tone, then this activity is the perfect one for your family. The humming game helps your children learn how to listen intently to tones they hear. Start by humming one note and then ask each child to hum the same note. Keep humming until everyone is humming the right tone in unison. Then, choose another note and start all over again. You can designate a leader for each round, too, and escalate the notes to extremely high tones or low tones to prompt some giggles.

○ MAKE MAGNETIC COOKIE SHEETS

AGES 6–8

If you don't have an activity bag for your next road trip, then this activity using household items is a lifesaver. Before heading out for your next vacation, gather up a few cookie sheets and magnets from the fridge to entertain the kids. While driving along, place a cookie sheet on each child's lap. Then, distribute the magnets and let them arrange them in various shapes. If you have plain magnets, bring a page of stickers so that your children can decorate the magnets too. This can also turn into a collaborative activity where one child starts to create a shape or design with the magnets and then passes the cookie sheet to another child to add his or her personal touch to the final product. If you have letter magnets, use those to make words or phrases.

○ DRAW A MAP OF YOUR SCHOOL

AGES 6-12

Put a fresh twist on your back-to-school planning with this activity that utilizes your kids' creativity and sense of direction. Before heading off for the first day of school, tour the grounds (with permission of the principal) and help your children create a map of the school grounds and buildings. The object of the project is to have each child draw a map of what they see. For example, start with a diagram of the school's perimeter and then have the kids label the playground, cafeteria, gym, or their homeroom classroom. They can also draw trees, bushes, and playground equipment. Once the maps are finished, challenge your children to use them the first day of school or even share with new children enrolled at the school to help them navigate the grounds.

○ CREATE CONVERSATION CARDS

AGES 6-12

If the chatter in your car during a road trip involves sibling squabbles, keep your kids talking in a productive manner with this activity. With just a bit of preparation before you leave town, you can spark conversations that are much more interesting and cordial. Before getting in the car, have each kid write down her favorite activities, hobbies, or interests. These can range from superheroes and animals to athletics and school activities. You can also search online for kids' conversation topics and add some of those options. Put each topic on a thin strip of paper, fold the sheets of paper, and enclose them in a ziplock bag. Then, when the squabbles begin, break out the bag of conversation topics and draw one out. Give the kids five minutes to discuss the topic before reaching for a new topic to spark a different conversation. Mom and Dad can join in the conversation, too, offering their thoughts about the topic or by even asking questions to keep the discussion interesting.

○ CONSTRUCT ALUMINUM FOIL ANIMALS

AGES 6–12
■■□

If you're planning a trip to the park or a long road trip, pack some aluminum foil to keep your kids entertained. With this common household product handy, your kids can let their imaginations thrive and keep their hands busy at the same time. Begin by supplying each child with a sheet of aluminum foil. Then, instruct them to make shapes, animals, or even tear the foil into strips to intertwine to make unique designs. From a swan or a duck to a triangle or cylinder, your kids can let their creativity thrive when bunching together the foil and forming unique objects. Let each child showcase their final product when you stop for a break on a road trip or while enjoying a picnic lunch in the park after a hike or jaunt on the playground.

○ PLAY ROAD TRIP BINGO

AGES 6–12
■□□

Bingo on a rainy day at home is fun, so take that game on the road too! This activity does require a bit of preparation before you embark on your journey, though. Gather a few sheets of paper and have the kids help you make bingo cards for the trip. Think about sights they may see while traveling, such as red leaves on trees, certain types of vehicles, farms, animals in pastures, specific highway signs, or busses on the road. Then, create a grid that looks like a bingo card and fill in each square with the suggestions, making each card different. Once you are on the road or traveling by train, make sure the kids have a clear view of their surroundings and encourage them to keep an eye out for items on their bingo card. Once they spot something on the card, have them place an X over the square. The first child to X out all four corners, a vertical line, a horizontal line, or a diagonal line wins the game.

○ MAKE TRAVEL LEGO KITS

AGES 6–10
■□□

Even if you are vacationing in the most exotic spot of the world, it's only natural for your kids to experience bouts of boredom. Keep them entertained in a hotel room, in the car, or while visiting family members' homes with this activity. Before leaving your home, grab a few small rectangular plastic containers. Gather up some Lego pieces from the playroom or your kids' rooms and evenly distribute different colored pieces into each container. While on the road or sitting in your hotel room, break out the Lego pieces and challenge your kids to create a shape, sculpture, or figurine with only the pieces found in their boxes. Once they have finished the project, encourage your children to mix and match their Lego pieces and build a larger sculpture together. You can even put different shapes and types of Lego pieces in the containers and have the children pass the boxes to the right or left to experiment with some new pieces.

○ CREATE A WORD FIND

AGES 8–12
■■■

The wordsmiths in your crew will love this activity. When prompting your kids to use their creativity and their knowledge, you can also create activities that keep them busy and learning while traveling. The object of this activity is to have each child create a word find for their friends or siblings. Give your children blank pieces of paper and tell them to write words vertically or horizontally with spaces in between each letter. Once they have written about ten to fifteen words, have them fill in the rest of the area with random letters. The overall structure should resemble a square of jumbled letters once they are finished. Then, have them pass their word find to another child, and challenge each child to find and circle all the words. The child who is able to find all words first wins that round.

○ PLAY A PAPER TOWEL MATCHING GAME AGES 8-12 ■■□

Grab a few empty paper towel rolls to use in the car on your next trip. Once you are on the road and the kids are getting restless, break out enough empty paper towel holders for each child. Randomly write letters on the paper towel holder with a pen or marker, covering several areas of the cylinder. Then, let each child examine the paper towel holder and numbers to try to memorize which numbers are on their designated structure. Collect the paper towel holders and have each child try to tell you the numbers on his or her assigned holder. The child who remembers the most numbers, wins that round.

○ HOST A HANGMAN GAME AGES 8-12 ■■□

Hangman is one of the easiest games to prepare for, and with just a pen and a piece of paper you can entertain your kids with this activity just about anywhere. Whether you are standing in line at the store, navigating a lull during a game of bowling, or driving along the road, this game is the ideal distraction from electronics. Start by drawing a horizontal line at the top of the page and then a vertical line down the center. This serves as the primary structure. Then, think of a phrase or word and mark blank spaces for each letter so your children can try to guess the word while guessing letters. Each child gets a chance to guess a letter, and if it is correct, fill in the spaces with the letter, but if it is incorrect, start by drawing a man's face. With each incorrect letter, draw additional parts of the man that include the body, arms, and legs. The object of the game is for the children to guess the word or phrase before the man's body is completely drawn.

Index